A Traveler's Guide to
MICHIGAN WINERIES CIDERIES & MEADERIES

LAURIE ROSE

THUNDER BAY
P R E S S

A Traveler's Guide to Michigan Wineries, Cideries & Meaderies
Published by Thunder Bay Press
West Branch, MI
thunderbaypressmichigan.com

Photographs by Laurie Rose
Maps by Josh Buhlman
Cover and Interior Design by Diane Kolak, Page 9 Design

ISBN 9781933272702

Notice: The information in this book is true and complete to the best of our knowledge. It is offered without guarantee on the part of the author or Thunder Bay Press. The author and Thunder Bay Press disclaim all liability in connection with the use of this book.

Other Guidebooks by Laurie Rose
A Guide to 199 Michigan Waterfalls
A Traveler's Guide to 116 Michigan Lighthouses
A Traveler's Guide to 100 Eastern Great Lakes Lighthouses
A Traveler's Guide to 116 Western Great Lakes Lighthouses

To Masina and Alex,
my heart and soul

Introduction

I visited my first Michigan winery when I was in my forties. A group of teachers were going, and I finally decided to tag along. I had avoided these trips in the past. I wasn't a wine person, and even if I did have a few favorite wines that I brought out for special occasions, that didn't exactly make me an aficionado. But I liked my friends, and agreed to what I thought would be an awkward and uncomfortable afternoon, made less so by being in their company.

At the first winery, we were greeted by a beautiful golden retriever. That's when I began to realize that my preconceived notions about wineries was completely off the mark. The formal atmosphere and judgmental looks were nowhere to be found. When I hesitantly told the person guiding our tasting that I only liked sweet wines, she was inviting rather than dismissive. She insisted she would find something that I liked, and she did. It was an eye-opening afternoon.

We visited a nice selection of my friends' favorites, and I was completely taken by the beautiful settings, unique architecture, and fascinating people. I thought I knew a lot about Michigan already. I had written a travel guide to Michigan waterfalls, and followed it up a few years later with a guide to Michigan lighthouses. I had traveled extensively throughout the state, but had somehow missed these unique attractions due to my wildly incorrect assumptions. And I didn't want anyone else to make the same mistake. So then I knew what the focus of my next guidebook would be. I would write about Michigan wineries.

I immediately began creating lists, poring over maps, and Googling for hours. In the summer of 2019, I began visiting wineries and taking photos. I noticed that many wineries also created hard cider, so I added cideries to my list. Meaderies quickly followed. By the end of the year, I was burned out, and decided that I'd take a few months off to organize, and return to the battle in the spring. But 2020 brought a battle of a different sort, and created an 18-month unanticipated sabbatical in my research. In 2021, I revised my list to include all of the changes the previous year had brought. Several wineries had closed, several more had sprung up, and many had updated during their own hiatus. By the end of the year, I had visited nearly 200 wineries, cideries, and meaderies in the state. It's a fluid list, and I hope to update it regularly.

I want this book to be the catalyst for your own day trips, something that intrigues you enough to get you on the road to some of Michigan's great destinations. I tell you where they are, what they look like, and how to contact them. Then I send you on your way. The history of the place is rarely included, as are any awards or critiques of the wines themselves. If you are looking for the nitty-gritty, I want you to talk to the people who live it every day, from the owners to the servers. I couldn't begin to translate the love they have for the creations they offer. So browse through the book, dog-ear a couple pages, and go explore Michigan.

—Laurie Rose
June 2022

Acknowledgements

I would like to thank the following individuals without whose help this book would never have come to be—I love you all:

My husband Ross, for his willingness to drive hundreds of miles to make sure I get all the photos I will ever need

My daughter Masina, for her calm guidance, encouragement, and excellent navigation skills (sorry we ended up in Indiana once) and her insightful editing suggestions

My son Alex, for his unending support and encouragement, a whirlwind tour of the Grand Rapids area, and a tiny piece of writing advice which made all the difference

My daughter-in-law Samantha, for her exuberance, encouragement, and love of Merlot

My friend Kathy Splan, for showing me what I was capable of at the beginning in Leelanau, and providing a push at the end

My friend Tammy Ahearne, for inviting me to the wine-tasting trip that started this whole thing, and agreeing to a wild weekend of wineries in the Ludington area

My friend Louise Hofer, for bringing her unique brand of calm and capable, exactly what I needed and at the perfect time, all in the exciting environs of Detroit

Contents

Sault Ste. Marie

Escanaba

Petoskey

Alpena

Traverse City

Bay City

Flint

Grand Rapids

Detroit

Kalamazoo

SOUTHWEST

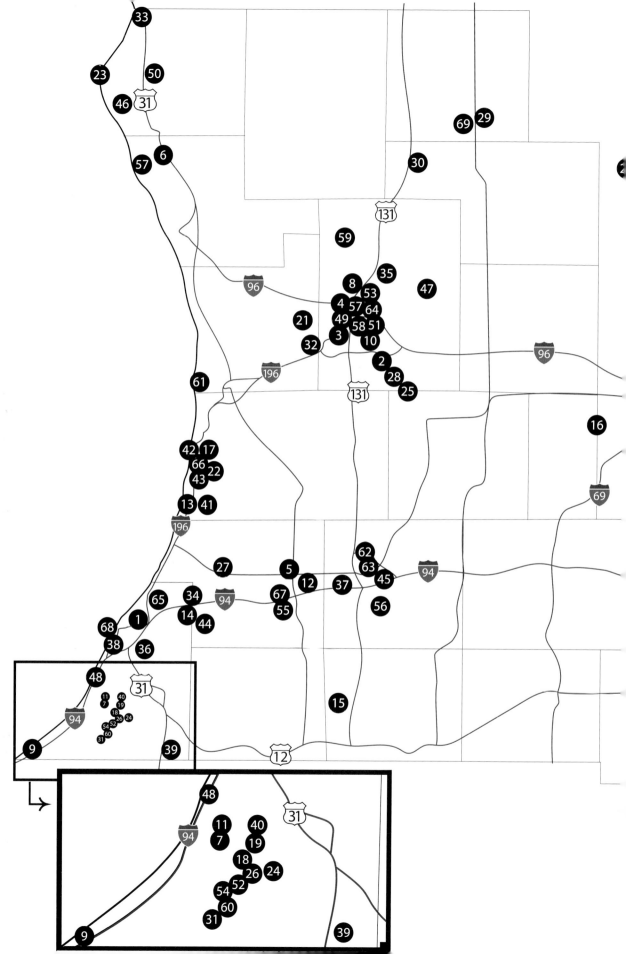

Southwest Michigan

12 Corners Vineyards

BENTON HARBOR · EST. 2013

T ucked away on a small rise, surrounded by vineyards and country fields, the expansive 12 Corners tasting room offers visitors their choice of vistas. The covered front porch stretches the width of the building, and a sunny patio overlooks the lush lawn brushing against the vineyard. The interior features an open design, exposed beams and a gorgeous window dominating the seating area, while the long L-shaped bar provides yet another place to enjoy yourself.

There is a small gift area, and Saturdays throughout the summer months bring live music to guests.

12 Corners also has tasting rooms in South Haven (511 Phoenix Rd.) and Grand Haven (41 Washington Ave., Suite 144).

POSSIBILITIES

Red/Rosé
Sweet Red Blend (Jane)
Cote du Rhone blend CDR (Betty)
Bordeaux Blend BDX (Evelyn)
Syrah Viognier (Shirley)
Merlot (Libby)
Cabernet Sauvignon
Cabernet Sauvignon Reserve
Rosé (Sue)

White
Pinot Gris (Ann)
Chardonnay (Hazel)
Sauvignon Blanc Lodi (Suzie)
Dry White Blend (Cornelia)
White Zinfandel

Sparkling
Lucky Bubbles Brut
Rosé (Nancy)
Peach (Jackie)

TASTINGS	TAKE HOME	RESERVATIONS
5 for $10	$7–$40	Walk in

VISIT
1201 N. Benton Center Rd. • Benton Harbor, MI 49022
269.927.1512 • info@12corners.com • 12corners.com
Open year-round

The 707 Winery

CALEDONIA · EST. 2021

One of Michigan's newest ventures, The 707 Winery and Brewery is easy to reach, tucked into a strip of businesses in the small town of Caledonia, about 15 miles southeast of Grand Rapids. There is a large tasting bar surrounded by barrel tables with plenty of room for a group of friends to try out the wares. Although they don't offer food, you are welcome to bring it in from outside and enjoy it with a glass of wine or beer.

POSSIBILITIES

Red/Rosé
Fireside Red
Cabernet Sauvignon
Merlot
Assignation

White
Cardonnay
Riesling

TASTINGS	TAKE HOME	RESERVATIONS
1 for $1	$15–$26	Walk in

VISIT

9175 Cherry Hill Ave. SE • Caledonia, MI 49316 • 616.710.0796
the707winery@gmail.com • facebook.com/707-Winery-and-Brewery
Open year-round

Adesanya Mead

GRANDVILLE · EST. 2020

Tucked into a nondescript but pretty strip mall, Adesanya Mead is home to a wide assortment of meads and several wines, along with craft beers, and visitors are sure to find something they enjoy. The tasting room is very light, with blonde wood tables and pale walls. The clean lines of the bar add to the minimal aesthetic, and everything combines to create a relaxing and welcome space. There are tables in front of the building, and food trucks are a weekly treat.

POSSIBILITIES

Mead
Alpha Gateway
Lyrical Graffiti
Now Slice
Phat Beats
Shiftless When Idle
The Illusion of Time
B3
Cyser and Doughnuts
Oak Aged Cyser and Doughnuts
Typical Situation
Zero Machine
Picture Puzzle Pattern Door
Tupelo Traditional
Fear of Illusion
Beauty in Chaos

Wine
Cabernet Sauvignon
Moscato
Pinot Noir
Pinot Grigio
Raspberry Peach Sangria
White Cranberry

TASTINGS
4 for $13

TAKE HOME
$25–$50

RESERVATIONS
Walk in

VISIT
3012 28th St. SW · Grandville, MI 49448
616.460.7404 · contact through website · adesanyamead.com
Open year-round

Arktos Meadery

GRAND RAPIDS · EST. 2014

As you push open the front door to Arktos, you'll enter into a world all its own, with hand-hewn beams, a fireplace, and a genuine invitation to relax among friends. The long bar stretches nearly the length of the room, and there are several tables towards the front as well as outdoor seating. A unique bonus space is found below, where table games are encouraged, and long evenings of D&D are common. They also sell miniatures, trading card games, and board games. Food trucks are on hand, and weekends offer live music, with occasional open mic nights.

POSSIBILITIES
Mead
Queen Bee
Enchanted Horse
Black Stripe
Three Bears
Fairy Godmother
Cricket Song
Great Bear

TASTINGS
$12–$20

RESERVATIONS
Walk in

VISIT
442 Bridge St. NW • Grand Rapids, MI 49504
616.419.0118 • info@arktosmeadery.com • arktosmeadery.com
Open year-round

B-52 Winery

PAW PAW · EST. 2019

Just a few miles north of Paw Paw, B-52 Winery and Lucky Girl Brewing share a spot at the corner of M-40 and M-43. They also share an overarching theme: honor our WWII veterans and the people who helped them. B-52 Winery has filled its space with women aviators, and their names and faces adorn many of the bottles they offer. The small blue tasting room offers plenty of seats at the bar, and several hightops to gather with friends. A few chairs in the front create a sunny spot to relax, and a larger outdoor seating area overlooks the parking lot.

B-52 is also the official tasting room for Henry's Heritage Blueberry Winery, a local establishment specializing in, of course, blueberry wines. Food options include charcuterie boards, quiche, dips, flatbreads, salads, and a coffee bar. If you're looking for something more substantial, cross the parking lot to Lucky Girl Brewing, which has a large menu specializing in authentic Mexican cuisine. They also offer a few meads and ciders.

POSSIBILITIES

Red/Rosé
Sweet Red Blend (Jane)
Cote du Rhone blend CDR (Betty)
Bordeaux Blend BDX (Evelyn)
Syrah Viognier (Shirley)
Merlot (Libby)
Cabernet Sauvignon
Cabernet Sauvignon Reserve
Rosé (Sue)

White & Sparkling
Pinot Gris (Ann)
Chardonnay (Hazel)
Sauvignon Blanc Lodi (Suzie)
Dry White Blend (Cornelia)
White Zinfandel
Lucky Bubbles Brut
Rosé (Nancy)
Peach (Jackie)

Blueberry
Blue Symphony
Barbara's Blessing
Bohemian Blue Rhapsody
Summer's Gold

TASTINGS	TAKE HOME	RESERVATIONS
6 for $10	$14–$24	Walk in

VISIT

34020 M-43 • Paw Paw, MI 49079

269.485.0074 · Contact through Facebook • facebook.com/B52Winery

Open year-round

Bardic Wells Meadery

MONTAGUE · EST. 2007

Bardic Wells Meadery is a local favorite, and has been bringing visitors around to the idea of mead as a much-loved drink for over a decade. As Michigan's longest licensed meadery, its attraction is both the friendly and funny staff and their quality meads. Although they don't serve food, you are invited to BYOF and

enjoy a game with friends, or just soak up the atmosphere. Although it might seem small from the outside, the L-shaped bar and several tables provide plenty of room to "party like a bard," as their motto says.

POSSIBILITIES

Mead
Bardic Red
Clutang
Apple Sass
Bardic Blue
Canoe Clu
Whippersnapper
Clu 22
Traditional
Bardic Gold
Black Clu
Brü Clu
Upside Down Clu
Apple Clu
Pyment
Root Fruit
Fuzzy Clu
Rhu Clu
Cordial Magic
Cherry Berry
Raz Clu
Bing Bang
Crane Fairy
Blue Bard
Cyser
Black Peggy

TASTINGS	TAKE HOME	RESERVATIONS
4 for $5	$11	Walk in

VISIT

8844 Water St. · Montague, MI 49437

616.837.8035 · mead@bardicwells.com · facebook.com/bardicwells

Open year-round

Baroda Founders Wine Cellar

BARODA · EST 2009

The small town of Baroda is home to a wine-loving family who has kept their heritage going strong, well into the second generation. Baroda Founders was created by Len Olsen, whose interest in wine making shaped his life. Len's son Gunner carries on his father's legacy.

The tasting room is spacious, with long wooden tables and plenty of room to relax. Photos honoring the family wine makers abound, and there's a cute collection of prints celebrating the wine-making monks of history and their products.

There is also a tasting room in St. Joseph (415 State St., 269.982.1115).

POSSIBILITIES
Red
Cabernet Franc
Chambourcin
Cuvée Rosé
Oh Hell Yeah! Red
Foch Rosé
Marquette
White
Lake Side Breeze
Luce Del Sole
Vidal Blanc Select Sweet Harvest
Seyval
Traminette
Fruit/Dessert
Green Apple
Antique Peach
Antique Cranberry
First Kiss
Smorleaux

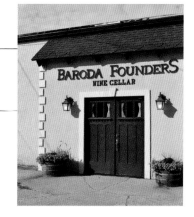

TASTINGS	TAKE HOME	RESERVATIONS
5 for $8	$12-$30	For groups of 8 or more

VISIT
8963 Hills Rd. • Baroda, MI 49101
269.426.5222 • founderswinecellar.com
Open year-round

Bier Distillery

COMSTOCK PARK · EST. 2013

If visiting a distillery was never on your radar, it's time to change that. This is the perfect place for an eclectic group of friends to meet; there's something for everyone, from their large selection of spirits and mixed drinks to their limited, but popular, line of wines. There is a small patio off the front of the building, with a few tables and shady umbrellas. Inside, there's plenty of room at the bar, and tables fill the open space. Their full menu offers many unique combinations, with an emphasis on authentic Dutch creations, such as the Beef Stew with apples and beer, and the Stroopwaffel Ice Cream to finish it off.

POSSIBILITIES

Wines
Brave
Niagara
Intrepid
Malicious
Sangria
Apple Cider
Pomegranate Chai

TASTINGS	TAKE HOME	RESERVATIONS
4 for $10	Spirits: $15-$35	Walk in

VISIT

5295 West River Dr. NE • Comstock Park, MI 49321

616.888.9746 • info@bierdistillery.com • bierdistillery.com

Open year-round

Black Dragon Meadery

NEW BUFFALO · EST. 2015

The brand new tasting room of Black Dragon Meadery shares space with its neighbor, Proměny Olive and Wine. The two combine to offer visitors not only a fine collection of meads, but an opportunity to taste international wines that have yet to be discovered by the mainstream. The meads are created using techniques that stay as true as possible to the original brewers, hence their motto "Return to the Olde Ways." The adjoining business also provides a showcase for imported olives, oils, and balsamic vinegars in its gift shop.

POSSIBILITIES

Mead
Wylde
Wyldeberry
Dragon's Blood
Blackberry
Magnum Mead Ale
The Razzler
Greenmead
Nectar of the Gods
Dazzling Raspberry Mead
Roasted Virgin Cherry Cyser
Blue Dragon Blueberry Cyser
Cyser
Wyldewood
Elderberry
Peach
Black
White
Red

TASTINGS	TAKE HOME	RESERVATIONS
5 for $10	$22-$28	Walk in

VISIT

910 W. Buffalo St., Suite 2 · New Buffalo, MI 49117

269.277.4874 · contact through website · blackdragonmeadery.com

Open year-round

Cascade Winery and Sierra Rose Cellars

GRAND RAPIDS · EST. 2003

Located in the center of a nondescript office building, Cascade Winery is a pleasant respite close to home for many. It also includes Sierra Rose Ciders, and they'll have a nice selection on tap for guests.

The curved bar provides a focal point, and there are a few tables nearby. A second room has plenty of tables to relax with your favorite offering, and a bit of privacy from the main tasting room.

POSSIBILITIES

Red/Rosé
Merlot
Rosso Grande
Cabernet Sauvignon
Cabernet Franc
Symphony Red

White
Chardonnay
Pinot Grigio
Traminette
Riesling
Gewürztraminer
Moscato

Fruit/Dessert
Apple
Black and Red
Blueberry
Cherry
Cranberry
Pear
Peach
Strawberry

Mead
Orange Spice Mead
Traditional Mead

Hard Cider
Peach
Raspberry
Pineapple
Cranberry
Cherry
Strawberry
Apple Pie

TASTINGS	TAKE HOME	RESERVATIONS
6 for $5	$11–$20	Group of 6 or more

VISIT

4665 Broadmoor Ave SE, Suite 135 • Grand Rapids, MI 49512

616.656.4665 • roger@cascadecellars.com • sierrarosecellars.com

Open year-round

Chill Hill Winery

BARODA · EST 2019

The colors of the Caribbean accent the tasting room of Chill Hill, and a definite beach vibe is going on. That's exactly what Ashley and Norma, granddaughter and grandmother, had in mind when they started the business together. Relaxed seating at the bar and surrounding tables invites you to settle in for a little bit of R&R amid a very friendly and happy atmosphere. When you leave, you'll feel like you've been at the lake all day!

POSSIBILITIES

Red/Rosé
Meritage
Countryside Red
Dockside Dan's
Catawba Rosé
Cherry Wine
Cranberry Blanc

White
Chardonnay
Pinot Gris
Dry Riesling
Semi-Sweet Riesling
Sweet Riesling

Hard Cider
Pineapple
Raspberry
April's Fool
The Crooked Campfire
Apple Crisp
Uncle Judd
Grapefruit
Peach

TASTINGS	TAKE HOME	RESERVATIONS
5 for $10	$15–$30	For large groups

VISIT

8986 First St. • Baroda, MI 49101

269.326.7173 • info@chillhill.net • chillhill.net

Open year-round

Cody Kresta Vineyard and Winery

MATTAWAN · EST. 2009

Imagine spending a peaceful afternoon relaxing on the patio, shady maples overhead and the sounds of a bubbling brook in the background. All this can be yours with a short drive down a country road to the distinctive red and white tasting room of Cody Kresta. Although the exterior resembles a barn, inside, the cozy décor feels Mediterranean, with walls of gold and burnt umber, and high top wrought iron tables running

the length of the room. The large patio on the back is furnished with several wrought iron seating areas, with a few umbrellas for the sunnier spots, and a beautifully landscaped water feature that attracts dragonflies and frogs during the summer.

There are several food events throughout the year, and occasionally live music on special weekends.

POSSIBILITIES

Red/Rosé
Skeet's Revelry
Cabernet Franc
Chambourcin
Pinot Noir
Rudy's Red
TriVina
Kresta Red
Mystique Red
Tradition
Rosé

White
Chardonnay
Pinot Gris
Riesling
Seyval Blanc
Vidal Blanc Ice Wine
Traminette
La Crescent
Portman's Legacy
Sauvignon Blanc
White Cabernet Franc

Fruit
Kresta Azure
Peach
Aurora Delight

TASTINGS	TAKE HOME	RESERVATIONS
4 for $8-$12	$11–$40	Walk in

VISIT

45727 27th St. · Mattawan, MI 49071

269.668.3800 · contact through website · codykrestawinery.com

Open year-round

Cogdal Vineyards and Little Man Winery

SOUTH HAVEN · EST. 2014

A long gravel drive leads guests to the gray and white tasting room of Cogdal Vineyards, also home to Little Man Winery. There is a large patio that offers views of the surrounding vineyard and the forest beyond, with a smaller covered area for shade lovers. Inside, the beautiful bar — created using hardwood from the property — can seat eight very comfortably, but the stone fireplace is much more enticing. There is a gift shop, as well as light snacks to see you through your visit.

POSSIBILITIES

Red/Rosé
Nana's Kiss
Reflection
Big Lake
Vision
Vin Rouge
Merlot
Cabernet Franc
VPS
South Beach
White
Whitecap
Charlie's Choice
Charlie's Bad Choice
Dry Riesling
Vin Blanc
Sweet Inspiration
Riesling LMS
North Beach
Speciality
Maple

TASTINGS	TAKE HOME	RESERVATIONS
5 for $7	$12–$23	Walk in

VISIT

7143 107th Ave · South Haven, MI 49090

269.637.2229 · littlemanwinery@gmail.com · cogdalvineyards.com

Open year-round

Contessa Wine Cellars

COLOMA · EST. 2002

The gray, chalet-style tasting room of Contessa Wine Cellars is situated at the crest of a small rise, embracing the rolling hills and sprawling vineyards of the surrounding area. A large deck provides a sunny place to enjoy the view, and stairs will lead you to another seating area, and a shady spot during those hot summer days.

In the tasting room, an oak bar invites visitors to slow down and enjoy the view from the two-story windows. Crystal chandeliers bring a sophisticated touch to the décor, but these aren't just your run-of-the-mill chandeliers: if you look closely, you'll realize their design is perfect for a vineyard.

POSSIBILITIES

Red/Rosé
Cabernet Franc
Merlot
Tre Tenores
Rosa d'amore
Lago Rosso
Dolce Vita
Prediletto Blush

White
Pinot Grigio
Chardonnay Reserve
Divino
Bianco Bello
Celeste

Fruit
Blueberry
Cherry

TASTINGS	TAKE HOME	RESERVATIONS
5 for $5	$11–$30	For groups of 8 or more

VISIT

3235 Friday Rd. · Coloma, MI 49038 · 269.468.5534

wine2015@contessawinecellars.com · contessawinecellars.com

Open year-round

23

Corey Lake Orchards

THREE RIVERS · EST. 1998

Perched at the crest of a small hill, Corey Lake Orchards has been creating wine, brandy, and cider for over 20 years. Currently, tastings are reserved for special weekends during their season, but bottles can always be purchased through the farm market, which includes produce as well as fresh baked goods, fresh cut flowers and their own sunflower field. The vineyard brushes up against the south of the parking area, providing a close look at the grapes throughout their growing season.

Because Corey Lake Orchards is a seasonal market, they will open in the late spring with the freshest of Michigan produce, and end the year in the fall, when they invite visitors to pick their own apples and grapes. Take home a bushel or two; maybe you could begin a wine tradition all your own.

POSSIBILITIES

Fruit
Double Cherry
Peach

Cider
Standard Sweet
Brunch
Blueberry
Preach
Standard Semi-Sweet
Standard Dry

Brandy
Apple
Bosc Pear
Bartlett Pear
Cherry
Peach
Double Distilled Niagara
Grappa

TASTINGS	TAKE HOME	RESERVATIONS
Occasionally	Wine: $11–$13	Walk in
	Brandy: $28–38	

VISIT

12147 Corey Lake Rd. • Three Rivers, MI 49093

269.244.5690 • coreylakeorchards@gmail.com • coreylakeorchards.com

Open seasonally

Country Mill Orchard and Winery

CHARLOTTE · EST. 2002

When the leaves start to turn, and change is in the air, head over to Country Mill Orchard and Winery for everything autumn. Although their wine tasting bar is very small, if you're looking for fruit wines, stop in. Built as most farm markets are, it's a seasonal building, with a few smaller areas of foods, wines, and everything fresh and lovely. Their "Cider Bar," a small restaurant within the building, offers visitors nachos and hotdogs, apple dumplings and mini pies. Fall activities include hay rides, apple and pumpkin picking, and even an apple cannon.

POSSIBILITIES
Hard Cider
Blueberry Apple Wine
Cherry Apple Wine
Dry Apple Wine
Maple Syrup Apple Wine

TAKE HOME	RESERVATIONS
$10	Walk in

VISIT
4648 Otto Rd. · Charlotte, MI 48813
517.543.1019 · mail@countrymill.com · countrymillfarms.com
Open seasonally

Crane's Pie Pantry and Winery

FENNVILLE · EST. 2014

Although the atmosphere inside Crane's revolves around their delicious edible offerings — apple butter and gouda toast, spicy chicken melts, and even a "pie flight" — they are definitely not putting their wine- and cider-making skills in a back corner. Just a few years after starting their hard cider endeavor, they won the prestigious honor of World's Best Flavored Cider for their Apple Cherry Hard Cider at the World Cider Awards in 2017. The accolades kept coming.

Inside, the two large seating areas for their restaurant helps manage visitors to the small tasting bar. Choose your favorite and order lunch. Bottles are available for purchase in their shop, which also offers a tempting assortment of all things sweet.

They also have a tasting room in Holland - Crane's in the City (11 East 8th St.)

POSSIBILITIES

Red/Rosé
Montage
The Homestead
Merlot

White
Sauvignon Blanc
Pinot Grigio
Dry Riesling
Seyval Blanc
Riesling

Fruit
Blueberry
Cherry

Cider
The Nepotist
Perry
Dry Apple
Blueberry
Cherry
Semi-sweet Apple

TASTINGS	TAKE HOME	RESERVATIONS
4 for $5	$20–$30	Walk in

VISIT
6054 124th Ave. • Fennville, MI 49408
269.561.2297 • contact@cranespiepantry.com • cranespiepantry.com
Open year-round

Dablon Vineyards & Winery

BARODA · EST. 2009

From the outside, the industrial architecture of the Dablon tasting room is all concrete and metal. But once you climb the stairs to the entrance, you're surrounded by dappled sunlight and a spacious veranda, the perfect place to relax. Inside, the curved marble bar welcomes visitors, and the large sitting room beyond is lit with floor-to-ceiling windows overlooking the vineyard.

Groups are limited to 12 visitors. Sundays you can enjoy a glass of your favorite while listening to a bit of live music, and there are occasional movie nights to enjoy with friends. No one under 21 is allowed on the premises.

POSSIBILITIES

Red/Rosé
Merlot
Carmenere
Cabernet Sauvignon
Tannat
Syrah
Pinot Noir
Cabernet Sauvignon Merlot Blend
Petit Verdot
Malbec
Estate Red Blend
Cabernet Franc
Producer's Cut
Music Box Matinee Red
Cabernet Sauvignon Reserve
Pinot Noir Rosé

White
Estate White Blend
Unoaked Chardonnary
Riesling
Sweet Riesling
Moscato
Pinot Grigio
Traminette
Chardonnay
Music Box Pinot Gris
Music Box Sweet Seyval Blanc

TASTINGS	TAKE HOME	RESERVATIONS
5 for $15	$17–$50	For groups of 8 or more

VISIT

111 W. Shawnee Rd. • Baroda, MI 49101

269.422.2846 • tastingroom@dablon.com • dablon.com

Open year-round

Domaine Berrien Cellars

BERRIEN SPRINGS · EST. 2001

Row upon row of grape vines greet visitors in search of Domaine Berrien Cellars tasting room. Following the long drive towards the unassuming blue and white building, you'll soon find yourself surrounded by the peaceful ambiance of farmland and forest beyond.

Inside, the tasting room itself is small but inviting, and a large veranda off the back offers plenty of room to stretch out and enjoy the sun. Windows in the tasting room overlook the production floor, and a gallery runs along one length of the building for a closer look at the wine-making process.

POSSIBILITIES

Red/Rosé
Pinot Noir
Cabernet Franc
Lemberger
Wolf's Prarie Red
Merlot
Cabernet Sauvignon
Crown of Cabernet
Syrah
Red Satin
Grandma's Red

White
Chardonnay
Oaked Marsanne
Riesling
Vignoles
Garden Party White

Dessert
Cabernet Franc Ice Wine

TASTINGS	TAKE HOME	RESERVATIONS
5 for $10	$12–$40	For groups of more than 6

VISIT

398 E. Lemon Creek Rd. • Berrien Springs, MI 49103

269.473.9463 • winery@domaineberrien.com • domaineberrien.com

Open year-round

Eastman's Forgotten Ciders

WHEELER · EST. 2015

The tasting room for Forgotten Ciders sits on the old homestead, surrounded by acres of orchards, and inviting visitors to sit a spell. They have stewardship of over a thousand different varieties of apple in their orchards, which gives them lots of options in developing their ciders. The bar is small, and there are a few tables inside, but seating areas nestle up against the exterior, with an overhang to protect from sun or rain. The red-sided, gray-shingled structure looks like another outbuilding, but much prettier and more enticing. The lush grass surrounding it provides ample room for any extra guests who can't find a seat indoors or on the porch.

If you can't make it to the tasting room on Saturday afternoon, you might be able to catch them at the Midland Farmer's Market from 7–1 on Saturday mornings, May to October.

POSSIBILITIES
Hard Cider
Out on a Limb
Private Stash
Opportunity Knocks
Cinnister
The Mad Russian

A Traveler's Guide to Michigan Wineries, Cideries, and Meaderies

TASTINGS	TAKE HOME	RESERVATIONS
4 for $6	$10–$18	Walk in

VISIT

1058 W. Midland-Gratiot County Line Rd. • Wheeler, MI 48662

773.428.9000 • forgottenciders@gmail.com

facebook.com/EastmansForgottenCiders

Open year-round

Farmhaus Ciders

HUDSONVILLE · EST. 2015

Surrounded by woods and just a stone's throw from the original white clapboard farmhouse, visitors to Farmhaus Cider can count on a friendly and inviting atmosphere, like coming home. The tasting room is inside their production facility, and although the bar is small, there's plenty of seating to enjoy a sip of one of the best ciders around. John, the owner, is the founder and president of the Michigan Cider Association, and his love for the craft is apparent as he welcomes guests and introduces them to his product.

They have a cute gift shop next to the tasting room with plenty of seating outdoors, which includes a fire pit and food trucks on Friday and Saturday through the summer and fall months.

POSSIBILITIES

Hard Cider
Sweater Weather
Lake Effect Blush
Lake Effect Zest
Daily Dry
Midwest Nice
Brunch
Punch Bowl Sangria
The Cucumber One
Skinny Dip Bloom
Skinny Dip Squeeze

TASTINGS
Flight: $8

TAKE HOME
4-pack of cans: $14

RESERVATIONS
Walk in

VISIT
5025 Stanton St. • Hudsonville, MI 49426
616.920.1867 • info@farmhauscider.com • farmhauscider.com
Open year-round

Fenn Valley Vineyards & Wine Cellar

FENNVILLE · EST. 1973

A large portico greets visitors to Fenn Valley Vineyards, providing seating areas sheltered from the elements and embellished by vines draping down from above. Inside, the tasting room is expansive, with a large bar and additional seating in a separate area, away from the gift shop. Moving beyond the bar, you can see the inner workings of the wine-making process from a gallery which looks down onto the production floor. Tours of the vineyard or cellars (depending on the weather) are $10, and they offer a private tour in the fall for up to 22 visitors.

Outside the tasting room, there are plenty of picnic tables, some with umbrellas, and a beautiful view of the green barn. The vineyard is just at the end of the lawn, angling off into the distance. It provides a beautiful backdrop to the Thursday night musical entertainment. Bring your lawn chairs, and relax with a glass of your favorite on a summer evening.

TASTINGS	TAKE HOME	RESERVATIONS
7 for $5	$9–$32	Walk in

VISIT

6130 122nd Ave. • Fennville, MI 49408

269.561.2396 • winery@fennvalley • fennvalley.com

Open year-round

POSSIBILITIES

Red/Rosé
Capriccio
Brairwood Red
Lakeshore Ruby Red
Meritage
Lakeshore Sunset
Brianwood Blush
Nouveau
Vino Rosé

White
Lakeshore Demi-Sec
Pinot Grigio
Briarwood White
True Chardonnay
Riesling
Vino Blanco
Traminette
Dry Traminette
Sweet Riesling
Classic Chardonnay
Lake Harvest Vignoles
Dry Riesling
Moscato
Sauvignon Blanc
Sonata

Specialty/Dessert
42 Ice Wine
Party Sangria
Mulled Wine
Classic Port
Bubbling Demi-Sec
Sparkling Riesling
Bubbling Rosé
Premier Cuvée

The Fox Barn

SHELBY · EST. 2008

Housed inside a venerable old barn on the family farm, the tasting room of The Fox Barn is filled with interesting visuals, from the post-and-beam work supporting the roof, to the displays surrounding their specialty wines. One of those specialties, Odd Fox, is an asparagus wine which they are only brave enough to offer on — of course — odd years. It corresponds to the local Asparagus Festival the second weekend in June, but be prepared — it sells out fast!

The tasting bar serves eight comfortably, but there is a large seating area outside, with plenty of chairs and tables, some covered by a pavilion. You can enjoy views of the working farm and the vineyard across the road. On Friday evenings in the summer, live music sets a festive mood. They offer a nice charcuterie, as well as cheesy dips and crackers.

POSSIBILITIES

Red/Rosé
Driftwood Red
Harvest Red
Harvest Rosé

White
Traminette
Harvest White
Silver Lake Sunset

Fruit
Harvest Cherry
Harvest Blueberry
Harvest Peach
Harvest Apple

TASTINGS
Flight: $7

TAKE HOME
$11–$21

RESERVATIONS
Walk in

VISIT
500 S. 18th Ave. • Shelby, MI 49455
231.861.8050 • info@thefoxbarn.com • foxbarnwinery.com
Open seasonally

Free Run Cellars

BERRIEN SPRINGS · EST. 2006

Nestled in a grove of oaks and brushing up against the vineyard, Free Run Cellars tasting room is a countryside retreat. Long tables bump up against a row of windows for a beautiful view of the greenery beyond. Outside, sitting areas provide a shaded respite from the worries of the day. Relax beside the still pond, or stay on the veranda and admire the vineyard. They also offer a charcuterie for those who would like something to nibble on.

There is also a tasting room in Union Pier (9185 Union Pier Road), which has offerings from Round Barn and Tabor Hill wineries as well.

POSSIBILITIES

Red/Rosé
Pinot Meunier Rosé
Pinot Noir
Lemberger
Syrah
Meritage
Rosso

White
Sauvignon Blanc
Fusion
Pinot Gris
Pinot Blanc
Dry Riesling
Mezzo
Gewürztraminer
Valvin Muscat

TASTINGS	TAKE HOME	RESERVATIONS
3 for $12	$18 to $50	For 8 or more

VISIT

10062 Burgoyne Rd. · Berrien Springs, MI 49103
269.815.6885 · hello@FreeRunCellars.com · freeruncellars.com
Open year-round

Glass Creek Winery

HASTINGS · EST. 2012

Tucked away in a secluded spot just west of Hastings, Glass Creek Winery offers a friendly destination for wine lovers, and beer lovers as well. They've also expanded into the micro brewery niche, so there is something here for everyone. The tasting room has a long bar, and a large seating area both inside and out. Stone decorated arches give it a Mediterranean feel, with plenty of room for all your friends.

Take a glass outside for sun or shade, as a long, covered porch runs the length of the building.

POSSIBILITIES
Red/Rosé
Old World Red
Malbec
Glass Creek Red
Cabernet Sauvignon
Hippy Kitty Red
Sangiovese
Concord
Lakeside Red
Merlot
White
Niagara
Seyval/LaCrosse
Riesling
Muscat
Dragon's Lair Chardonel
Gewürztraminer
Pinot Blanc
Chardonnay
Traminette
Lakeside White
Medieval Vino
Fruit
Blueberry
Coconut/Pineapple
Peach
Summer Sensation
Wild Berry
White Cranberry
Glass Creek Sangria
Black Cherry
Apple
Tropical Wave
Plum

TASTINGS
$1 each

TAKE HOME
$13–$29

RESERVATIONS
Walk in

VISIT
450 N. Whitmore Rd. • Hastings, MI 49058
269.986.6473 • glasscreekwinery@live.com • glasscreekwinery.com
Open year-round

Gravity Winery

BARODA · EST. 2011

The blue and white tasting room for Gravity Winery is an invitation just waiting to be opened. Inside, the blue theme is continued with blocks of color and a large bar. Plenty of tables surround the bar, but you'll want to take yours on the covered deck, weather permitting, and enjoy the beautiful setting on a hilltop above their private lake. Take a stroll through their nicely landscaped areas, or walk down to the lake. Just be sure you have the energy to climb back up the hill!

There is plenty of room here, but they request no groups larger than 15, so that they may better serve you. In summer, Sunday offers live music and a few light snacks.

There is also a tasting room in South Haven (512 Phoenix St.).

POSSIBILITIES

Red/Rosé
Equation
Pull
Irresistable Red
Pinot Noir Rosé Bubbly
Merlot
Rosé
Chocolate Cherry Dessert

White
Chardonnay
Pinot Gris
Traminette
Attraction
Elevation
Liquid Gold
Michigan Magnetism

Fruit
Blueberry

Sparkling Cider
Green Apple
Cherry Chipotle
Cinnamon Maple
Mango Berry

TASTINGS	TAKE HOME	RESERVATIONS
6 for $13	$13–$29	Walk in

VISIT

10220 Lauer Rd. • Baroda, MI 49101

269.471.9463 • info@gravitywine.com • gravitywine.com

Open year-round

A Traveler's Guide to Michigan Wineries, Cideries, and Meaderies

Great Mead Hall and Brewing

BANGOR · EST. 2016

In downtown Bangor, there's a place to quench your thirst for mead, and also try your hand at a unique pastime — axe throwing. The large interior of the Great Mead Hall provides the space for a throwing cage, and even sports a league. If you're hesitant to try your skill, you can still watch the action from the long bar stretching the length of the room, and test out their newest concoctions. Axe throwing is $20/hour, weekends only, and reservations are requested.

POSSIBILITIES

Mead
Old Scrumpy
Herminator
MZ Beuregarde
King Alcinous
Óðrerir
John Lake
Wahta Ohses
Maillard
Kraneia
Sibley
Ida's Blood

TASTINGS	TAKE HOME	RESERVATIONS
5 for $5	$20	Walk in

VISIT

215 W. Monroe • Bangor, MI 49013

269.427.0827 • speakeasyinbangor@gmail.com • greatmeadhall.net

Open year-round

Grimsby Hollow Meadery

MIDDLEVILLE · EST. 2016

Grimsby Hollow occupies space in a nondescript strip mall in Middleville, but that is the only ordinary thing about it. Their bar is small, but they have plenty of room at the tables spread throughout the space. They are all about the romance of the mead story, and everything comes together to create the most welcoming vibe. In addition to their meads, they also offer creative paninis, delicious desserts, non-alcoholic craft soda and gourmet loose leaf tea from Vampyre Tea Company.

Watch for their educational series "Drink Mead, Learn Things." Buy a ticket — they'll sell out fast — and learn about saber fighting, the warriors of Ireland, or ornamental landscaping. Guests 12 years old and above are welcome, as long as they're accompanied by an adult over 21.

POSSIBILITIES

Meads

The Beekeeper
The Midsummer Night
Raven Heart
Raspberry Malone
Becky Malone
A Date with a Pirate
Villains Need Love, Too
Cobra Chai
Mystique
Luchador
Blue Aurora
Valkyrie

TASTINGS	TAKE HOME	RESERVATIONS
4 for $11	$26–$30	Walk in

VISIT

4525 N. M-37, Suite E • Middleville, MI 49333

616.916.2418 • contact@grimsbyhollow.com • grimsbyhollowmeadery.com

Open year-round

Come ye wayward souls, the misfits, the creators, the daring dreamers, with hearts afire... Enter the Hollow

Gwin Girls Winery

REMUS · EST. 2019

The entrance to Gwin Girls Winery is well marked; just follow the long dirt drive to the building with the purple door, and you're there. The lawn, surrounded with fields and woods to the back, provide plenty of room to stretch out and enjoy the sun. There is a small covered patio in the front which offers shelter from inclement weather. In the back, a large mural provides a cute photo op. Inside, the country feel of Gwin Girls is highlighted in the colorful repurposed furniture, informal seating areas, and twin garage doors that open to bring the countryside indoors. They offer a charcuterie tray, as well as sandwiches, wraps and dips.

POSSIBILITIES

Red/Rosé
Imagine
Mysterious Rosé
Tribby Red

White
Perfect White
Riesy's Sunny Day
Just Delightful

Hard Cider
Blue on Black
Red Ryder
Rhett
Peachy Keen
Sassy Razz
Smitty

TASTINGS
5 for $5

TAKE HOME
$13–$15

RESERVATIONS
Walk in

VISIT
3600 Nine Mile Rd. • Remus, MI 49340
517.282.7100 • gwingirlswinery@gmail.com • gwingirls.com
Open seasonally

Heavenly Vineyards

MORLEY · EST. 2012

Tall maples protect the bronze and yellow façade of Heavenly Vineyards, providing deep shade for their patio and entranceway. Seating areas are scattered near the trees, providing the perfect place to relax with your favorite offering. Indoors, a heavy bar spans the width of the room, and there's plenty of additional seating. They have started to experiment with brewing as well as wine-making, and everything is made on site. On occasion, they offer an "Uncork & Paint" experience, which is a great activity to enjoy with all your wine friends.

POSSIBILITIES

Red/Rosé
Rusty Red
VCR

White
Vignoles
Big G

Fruit/Specialty
Rhubarb
Lemon
Jase
Viridity
Sapphire
Trinity
Demitasse

TASTINGS	TAKE HOME	RESERVATIONS
4 for $5	$11–$19	Walk in

VISIT

15946 Jefferson Rd. • Morley, MI 49336 • 616.710.2751
heavenlyvineyards@gmail.com • heavenlyvineyards.weebly.com
Open year-round

Hickory Creek Winery

BUCHANAN · EST. 2006

The big red barn of Hickory Creek's tasting room dominates the fields which surround it. Built with the intention of housing a winery, most of the interior is dedicated to production, but they've reserved a small room for visitors, with a long bar which looks out over the production floor. The friendly owners and staff will make you feel right at home, so after your tasting, choose your favorite glass and head outside; a towering oak and apple tree provide the perfect shady spot to relax. There's even a tire swing if you want to relive your childhood a bit.

POSSIBILITIES

Red/Rosé
Marquette Nouveau
Cabernet Franc
Syrah
Syrah Reserve
Merlot
Cabernet Sauvignon

White
Pinot Blanc
Chardonnay
Seyval Blanc
Pinot Grigio
Blue Star White
Heirloom Apple

TASTINGS	TAKE HOME	RESERVATIONS
5 for $10	$19–$31	6 or more, call ahead

VISIT
750 Browntown Rd. • Buchanan, MI 49102 • 269.422.1100
info@hickorycreekwinery.com • hickorycreekwinery.com
Open year-round

Hudsonville Winery

HUDSONVILLE · EST. 2009

From the entrance the red and white tasting room of Hudsonville Winery seems tiny, but once inside, the building extends much farther back, giving visitors plenty of room at the long bar and large seating area, as well as the additional seating areas outside overlooking the pond. This is also home to Pike 51 Brewery, as well as a restaurant. Just the place to go when you have a group of unique tastes. Wine, beer, mead, a juicy burger, what else is there?

Maybe frozen wine? Hudsonville offers several selections to cool you off, as well as a frozen flight of four for $10. If you are visiting with a group, call ahead and speak to a manager.

POSSIBILITIES

Red/Rosé
Shiraz
Tres Amici
Bruno

White
Chardonnay
Pinot Grigio
Gewürztraminer

Fruit/Dessert
White Cranberry
Hudsonberry
Green Apple
Peach
Raspberry
Black Cherry
Blueberry
Acai

Mead
Cherry Bliss
Blueberry Jamboree Melomel

TASTINGS	TAKE HOME	RESERVATIONS
Vary	$10–$30	Walk in

VISIT

3768 Chicago Dr. • Hudsonville, MI 49426
616.662.4589 • rsnider@hudsonvillewinery.com • hudsonvillewinery.com
Open year-round

Jomagrha Vineyards and Winery

PENTWATER · EST. 1999

Guarded by a row of pines along the road, a short driveway leads to the Jomagrha tasting room and the large white barn nearby. All wines are made on site, with local grapes, including their own. There is a covered patio to sit and enjoy a glass of your favorite wine, surrounded by the diminutive vineyard just a few feet away. At the end of each row, roses offer up a beautiful display.

POSSIBILITIES

Red/Rosé
Cab Franc/Chambourcin
Bison Red
Marquette
Old Man Red
Black Cherry Vidal
Sweet Berry Red
Labrusca

White
Aurora
Lakeshore White
Pinot Gris
Old Lady White
West Shore White
Cayras
Three Sister Blush
Cayuga White
Niagara

TASTINGS	TAKE HOME	RESERVATIONS
5 for $5	$13–$15	Walk in

VISIT

7365 S. Pere Marquette • Pentwater, MI 49449

231.869.4236 • contact through website • jomagrha.com

Open seasonally

Karma Vista Vineyards

COLOMA · EST. 2002

Perched on top of a hill near the small town of Coloma, Karma Vista tasting room is surrounded by vineyards which ultimately lead to the wines you'll taste. A small sitting area on the front porch provides a secluded perch to enjoy the vineyard, which begins just at the end of the lawn. Inside, the dark blue of the tasting room and gift shop emphasizes the sprawling vista surrounding it. Enjoy the view from the long stone bar, or bask in the sunshine on the spacious deck.

POSSIBILITIES

Red/Rosé
Reserve Syrah
Grand Sun Syrah
Reserve Merlot
Cabernet Sauvignon
Stone Temple Pinot
Surrealist Pinot
Marquette
Cote D'Loma
Devil's Head Red
Watusi Red
Gunzan Rosé

White
Cha Cha Chardonnay
Sauvignon Blanc
SoCo Grigio
Valvin Muscat

Fruit/Sparkling
Peach Train
Cherri Amour

TASTINGS	TAKE HOME	RESERVATIONS
5 for $5	$9–$34	No groups over 6, no buses or limos

VISIT

6991 Ryno Rd. · Coloma, MI 49038

269.468.9463 · info@karmavista.com · karmavista.com

Open year-round

Kayla Rae Cellars

ROCKFORD EST. 2012

Overlooking the Rogue River, Kayla Rae Cellars has a front row seat to the beauty the town has to offer. The cute brown and white building is just yards away from the walkways winding along the riverbank, and the dam overlook. The area is filled with small shops and eateries, making it the perfect place for an afternoon get-together.

The tasting room sports a stone bar, with an additional seating area up a few steps. Outside, a shady patio offers a tempting gathering spot on a sunny afternoon. Tastings are $1 per sample, and they offer a cheese and cracker tray accompaniment.

POSSIBILITIES

Red/Rosé
Pinot Noir
Malbec
Merlot
Cabernet Sauvignon
Depot Red
Winemaker's Red
Mirage
Syrah
Cabernet Franc Blush
White
Pinot Grigio
Sauvignon Blanc
Chardonnay
Riesling
Dam White
Muscato
Fruit/Dessert
Dam Red
Black Forest
Delight

TASTINGS	TAKE HOME	RESERVATIONS
$1 per sample	Wine: $13 to $18	Walk in
	Cider: $3 per can	

VISIT

31 Courtland St. • Rockford, MI 49341

616.951.7001 • roxanne@kaylaraecellars.com • kaylaraecellars.com

Open year-round

Lake Michigan Vintners

BENTON HARBOR · EST. 2014

There are exciting things happening at Lake Michigan College in Benton Harbor; students enrolled in their Wine & Viticulture Technology program have the opportunity to showcase their creations in their new on-campus tasting room. The Welch Center, on the north side of campus, is a large gray and burgundy building with a steel roof, dominating the small rise overlooking a pond and wooded area.

Inside, the long white bar offers plenty of space for tastings, and a covered deck off the back makes a quiet spot for friends to gather. They also offer cheese for pairings, and small plates.

POSSIBILITIES

Red/Rosé
Waters Edge
Cabernet Sauvignon
Pinot Noir
Red Hawk Red
Rosé

White
Pinot Gris
Chardonnay
Dry Riesling
Wavelength White
Riesling
Vin Doux

TASTINGS	TAKE HOME	RESERVATIONS
3 for $10	$12–$32	Walk in

VISIT

2774 East Empire Ave. • Benton Harbor, MI 49022 • 269.927.4731
info@lakemichiganvintners.com • lakemichiganvintners.com
Open year-round

Lawton Ridge Winery

KALAMAZOO EST. 2008

The cozy tasting room for Lawton Ridge is just a few miles west of Kalamazoo, and offers samples of several of their award-winning wines. Although the building is large, they also house their production facilities there, so they ask that you make reservations if you have a group of six or more visitors. A small gift selection is on display, and you can settle in with a glass of your favorite indoors or on their small patio.

On Wednesdays, a food truck is part of the celebration, and they switch out throughout the month to provide variety.

POSSIBILITIES

Red/Rosé
Two-Handed Red
AZO Red
Sweetheart Red
Lawton Ridge 3
Collage
Cranberry

White
Pinot Grigio
AZO White
Semi-Sweet Riesling
Traminette
Just Peachy

TASTINGS	TAKE HOME	RESERVATIONS
6 for $6	$15–$30	For 6 or more

VISIT

8456 Stadium Dr. • Kalamazoo, MI 49009 • 269.372.9463
chaltom@lawtonridgewinery.com • lawtonridgewinery.com
Open year-round

Lazy Ballerina Winery

ST. JOSEPH · EST. 2015

Downtown St. Joseph, just blocks from Silver Beach, is home to Lazy Ballerina Winery tasting room. The emphasis here is on fun, not fancy, and their relaxed and friendly vibe is very welcoming. There's plenty of room at the bar, and seating areas are scattered throughout. The owners of Lazy Ballerina enjoy surprising their visitors with something new each time they come in. It might be a wine & local cheese pairing, a showcase of handmade farmhouse-style décor to browse through, or the more creative pairings they have throughout the year.

There is also a Lazy Ballerina tasting room in Bridgman (4209 Lake Street).

POSSIBILITIES

Red/Rosé
Royale Rosé
Attitude Rosé
Pink Tutu
Concord Rosé
Cabernet Sauvignon
Barrel Rouge
Midnight Swan
Cavalier

White
Legs
White Swan
Pinot Grigio
Weko Beach White
Relevé Riesling
Nita's Niagara

Fruit/Sparkling
Cranberry
Single & Ready to Mingle
Anniversary Bubbly

TASTINGS
5 for $10

TAKE HOME
$10–$40

RESERVATIONS
For 8 or more

VISIT

321 State St. · St. Joseph, MI 49106

269.363.6218 · contact through website · lazyballerinawinery.com

Open year-round

Lehman's Orchard

NILES · EST. 2008

There are two places to sample the offerings of Lehman's Orchards, and neither is a traditional tasting room. They have a seasonal farm market near Niles which has a small spot for tastings, and a larger restaurant/brewery in Buchanan that offers flights of their cider and beer. Visitors to the very busy farm market can count on an entertaining afternoon spent picking fruit, from apples to strawberries and raspberries (all in the proper season, of course) and inside the market, there is an assortment of everything good. Homemade jams, honey, vinegars and other offerings line the shelves, as well as an assortment of their wines.

In Buchanan, Lehman's Orchard Brewery and Farmhouse (204 N. Red Bud Trail) is a full-menu restaurant with an emphasis on local produce. Guests can dine indoors or on the patio, near a small stream. The large building also houses a gift shop with plenty of those homemade attractions, including their wine, cider, beer and spirits.

POSSIBILITIES

Red/Rosé
Petit Syrah
Dornfelder
Bläufrankisch

White
Chardonnay
Traminette
Vignoles

Fruit
Concord
Honey Crisp Apple
Johnny Appleseed
Balaton Cherry
Pure Cherry
Pure Peach
Pure Pear

Hard Cider
Respberry Apple
Blueberry Apple
Farmhouse

TASTINGS
4 for $12

TAKE HOME
Wine $9 to $11
Cans/Cider $3 to $5

RESERVATIONS
Walk in

VISIT

2280 Portage Rd. · Niles, MI 49120

269.683.9078 · info@lehmansorchard.com · lehmansorchard.com

Orchard open seasonally · Restaurant open year-round

Lemon Creek Winery

BERRIEN SPRINGS · EST. 1984

On the banks of Lemon Creek (named after an ancestor of the current owner), a 165-year-old family farm is still standing strong. Today, the modern farm includes orchards and vineyards that attract visitors who want to pick their own fruit, shop at the farm market, and enjoy the wines on display in the tasting room nearby. The large tasting room offers a glimpse of the production facilities behind French doors just beyond the curved bar. Outdoors, you can relax at tables overlooking the beautiful creek, or use the generous outdoor picnic area on the shady lawn to sample some of the goodies from the farm market. Because they are an active farm, they can't allow pets.

Lemon Creek Winery also has a tasting room in Grand Haven (327 N. Beacon Rd., 616.844.1709).

POSSIBILITIES

Red/Rosé
Pinot Noir Rosé
Pheasant Run Red
Grand Lacs Rouge
Lighthouse Red
White
Chardonnay
Chardonnay Reserve
Sauvignon Blanc
Pinot Blanc
Dry Riesling
Semi-Dry Riesling
Pinot Grigio
Gewürztraminer
Sparkling/Specialty
Blanc de Blanc
Blanc de Noir
Ice Wine
Snow Moon
Blood Moon

TASTINGS	TAKE HOME	RESERVATIONS
5 for $15	$9–$40	For 7 or more

VISIT

533 E. Lemon Creek Rd. • Berrien Springs, MI 49103
269.471.1321 • lemoncreekwinery@gmail.com • lemoncreekwinery.com
Open year-round

A Traveler's Guide to Michigan Wineries, Cideries, and Meaderies

McIntosh Cellars

SOUTH HAVEN · EST. 2006

The tasting room for McIntosh Cellars is in a pretty gray farmhouse with a wraparound porch, surrounded by the orchards which will eventually be turned into all of the goodies you see inside. The bar is cozy, with room for nine comfortably, but there are plenty of tables on the nearby enclosed porch. Enjoy the warmth of the sunroom on a brisk autumn day, or venture out to the shady porch and enjoy your wine or a craft beer. There are also sitting areas spread out around the lawn. They all provide a lovely, relaxing view of the orchards.

There is a nice gift shop inside, with an eclectic mix of jewelry, items for wine lovers, and homemade fudge and cider donuts. Along with the sweet treats, the also have bread and cheese, and Friday night pizza. So shop, sip, and savor the relaxing atmosphere of a visit to the country.

POSSIBILITIES

Fruit
Golden Russet
Balaton Cherry
Pear
Peach
Apple Cinnamon
Strawberry
Blushing Bare
Cranberry
White Cranberry
Blueberry
Raspberry
Blackberry
Red & Black

Hard Cider
Apple
Perry
Iced Cider

TASTINGS	TAKE HOME	RESERVATIONS
4 complimentary	$14–$23	Walk in

VISIT

6431 107th Ave. • South Haven, MI 49090

269.637.7922 • contact through website • mcintoshorchards.com

Open year-round

Michigan Wine Company

FENNVILLE · EST. 2018

One of the newest wineries to make a name for themselves is the Michigan Wine Company, just a mile from the Lake Michigan shoreline. They offer award-winning ciders as well as a nice selection of reds and whites. The tasting room, with its red steel roof and contrasting gold wood siding, is at the end of a long drive which passes through the vineyard.

Inside, a semi-circular bar clad in rolled steel offers a good view of the surrounding fields, and the patio just outside. The wall of windows can be opened in the summer, letting in a cool breeze. There is plenty of seating both inside and out.

POSSIBILITIES

Red/Rose
Chancellor
Rosé of Cabernet
Frontenac Gris
Cab & Cab
Bubbley Rosé
Marechal Fosh
Barrel Reserve Marquette

White
Dry Hopped
White Blend
Seven Days
Bubbly Riesling
Traminette
K Vineyards Field Blend

Hard Cider
Grant Twp Dry Cider
Grant Twp Hop Cider

TASTINGS
4 for $10

TAKE HOME
$18 to $28

RESERVATIONS
For 6 or more

VISIT
6781 124 Ave. • Fennville, MI 49408 • 269.543.5011
michiganwinecompany@yahoo.com • michiganwineco.com
Open year-round

Modales Wines

FENNVILLE · EST. 2019

The blue and white steel-clad tasting room of Modales Wines is a true oasis in the midst of surrounding farmland and forest. Inside, a spacious bar curves out from the entrance, leading guests to the seating areas beyond. The open ceiling and plenty of windows offers up a relaxing atmosphere; a large covered patio wraps around two sides of the building with a sunny seating area beyond. The beautiful patio provides the perfect place to enjoy a fall afternoon or a summer sunset across the fields.

In the warmer months, Saturdays are filled with live music, and occasionally a paired wine tasting event is scheduled.

POSSIBILITIES

Red/Rosé
Lamastus Red Blend
Pinot Noir
Blaufrankish
Cabernet Franc
Chambourcin
Rosé

White
Herman Riesling
Pinot Blanc
Roth Riesling
Sauvignon Blanc
Chardonnay
Pinot Grigio
Sweet Riesling
Grüner Vetliner

Hard Cider
Seco Cider
Dulce Cider

TASTINGS
5 for $15

TAKE HOME
$14–$34

RESERVATIONS
Recommended

VISIT
2128 62nd St. • Fennville, MI 49408
269.722.3505 • sales@modaleswines.com • modaleswines.com
Open year-round

Moonrise Winery

WATERVLIET · EST. 2016

The tasting room of Moonrise Winery is protected by a vineyard rising on a hill behind it, and woods beyond. The pretty landscaping, filled with lots of colorful flowers, invites visitors to enjoy a glass outdoors, and revel in the views. Although they don't provide official tours, guests are welcome to explore the vineyard themselves, walk amongst the flower beds or climb the hill to a rewarding view. Inside, a generous bar dominates the room, but there are also tables alongside the windows and a nice back patio.

If you're a bit peckish, there are local cheese and sausage to be had, to go along with your favorite wine.

POSSIBILITIES

Red/Rosé
Merlot
Cabernet Franc
Cabernet Sauvignon
Heritage
Transition Red
Cabernet Franc Rosé
Concord Jack
Sweet Melissa

White
Chardonnay
Grüner Veltliner
Amore
Bainbridge
Feelin' Grü V
Ambrosia
Sangria

TASTINGS	TAKE HOME	RESERVATIONS
5 for $10	$12–$28	Walk in

VISIT

7785 Hill Rd. · Watervliet, MI 49098

269.468.4056 · moonrisewinery@gmail.com · moonrisewinery.com

Open seasonally

Norse Nectar Meadery

KALAMAZOO · EST. 2018

Since 2018, Norse Nectar Meadery has been celebrating the old ways, and providing a gathering place for those like-minded individuals to celebrate with them. There are open mic nights — both music and comedy — tarot on occasion, and weekly trivia nights. There is also a Sunday gathering of Communitas Paganus, where the pagan community can meet up.

Valhalla is the official tasting room for Norse Nectar, as well as City Union Brewery. Although they don't serve food, you are welcome to bring whatever you wish and make a night of it.

POSSIBILITIES

Mead
Holy Grail
Loki
Skadi
Dag the Wise
Dark Angel
Idunn
Tyr
Finn McCool

TASTINGS	TAKE HOME	RESERVATIONS
5 oz. pour for $5	$12	Walk in

VISIT

3408 Miller Rd. #309 • Kalamazoo, MI 49001

269.213.1578 • hunter@norsenectar • norsenectar.com

Open year-round

Oceana Winery & Vineyard

NEW ERA · EST. 1985

Bordered by vineyards on either side, a gravel drive leads to Oceana's unassuming tasting room; but don't let the size bother you. Personalities are larger than life here, and visitors can spend an enjoyable hour chatting with the staff, who love to talk about everything wine.

The tasting bar is small, perhaps four could stand together, but there are a few tables nearby. Outside, they have a nice sitting area nestled among the pines, with a view of the vineyard.

POSSIBILITIES

Red/Rosé
Pinot Noir Reserve
Red Mélanges
Oceana Red

White
Coastal Waltz
Chardonnay
Symphony
Minuet G Minor
Cayuga Jazz
Oceana White

Dessert
Enchanting Berries

TASTINGS	TAKE HOME	RESERVATIONS
5 for $5	$17–$23	Walk in

VISIT

4980 S. 52nd Ave. • New Era, MI 49446

231.343.0038 • contact through website • oceanawinery.com

Open seasonally

Painted Turtle Hard Cider

LOWELL · EST. 2015

The Red Barn Market, just north of Lowell, is home to the Painted Turtle Hard Cider tasting room. Inside you'll find not only award-winning ciders, but seasonal fruits, preserves, a large selection of ice cream concoctions, and a sizable menu of traditional diner fare. Something, simply put, for everyone.

Although there is no bar for tastings, there is plenty of seating at picnic tables both indoors and out. For animal lovers of all ages, there is a petting zoo with farm animals, as well as a play area. It's the perfect outing for a family afternoon.

POSSIBILITIES

Hard Cider
Traditional
Apple Crisp
Cozy Cabin
Humdinger Hopped
Java Vanilla
Heartseed Berry
Blueberry Bliss
Buzzin' Blackberry
Mango Lime
Sweet Cherry
Private Reserve Bourbon Barrel Aged

TASTINGS	TAKE HOME	RESERVATIONS
4 for $9	Cans: $7–$8	Walk in

VISIT

3550 Alden Nash Ave. NE • Lowell, MI 49331 • 616.987.3182
info@paintedturtlehardcider.com • paintedturtlehardcider.com
Open year-round

Peat's Cider Social

STEVENSVILLE · EST. 2017

If you have a taste for 1960s Americana, then I have just the place for you. Peat's Cider Social tasting room has found a home in a beautiful mid-century bowling alley, where you can enjoy the latest in hard cider creations while brushing up on your lane game. Retro design fills the interior, creating a nostalgic mood for visitors.

There is plenty of seating both inside and on the large outdoor patio. Visitors are welcome to bring their own food, or explore the delicious offerings of visiting food trucks. With a one hour lane rental for $25, Peat's is definitely a fun place to be.

POSSIBILITIES

Hard Cider
The Huntsman
The Apothecary
The Petal Pusher
The Matchmaker
The Birdwatcher
the Skipper
the Crush
Stay Flippy
Anime Running

TASTINGS	TAKE HOME	RESERVATIONS
6 for $16	4-pack cans: $16–$19	Walk in

VISIT

6201 Red Arrow Hwy • Stevensville, MI 49127

269.465.6814 • info@peatscider.com • peatscider.com

Open year-round

The People's Cider Co.

GRAND RAPIDS · EST. 2011

An homage to the working folks of Michigan, The People's Cider Co. recognizes not only the hard work that goes into every batch of cider, but the effort put forth by everyone each day who helps keep the country running. And what better place to end the day than in their cozy tasting room, relaxing with a favorite cider.

Long plank tables encourage groups to mingle, and the dark green walls soften the light and create a welcome atmosphere. Red stools line the bar and tables, providing a pop of color. There is additional seating outside, where a heater makes it an option even in the winter months. Food is available only occasionally, St. Patrick's Day for instance, but there are several eateries within walking distance that make this a popular post-dining destination.

POSSIBILITIES
Hard Cider
P.C.Co #1
Brick Street
People's Scrumpy
Sister Anne
Holiday Helper

TASTINGS
Flights $16–20

TAKE HOME
Cans: $5–$7

RESERVATIONS
Walk in

VISIT

539 Leonard St. NW, Suite B • Grand Rapids, MI 49504

616.427.4047 • thepeoplescider.com

Open year-round

Pux Cider

GRAND RAPIDS · EST. 2012

The relaxed, colorful atmosphere of Pux Cider is a nice contrast to the city beyond its doors. Weathered wood panels the bar and walls, and above, curved strips of old barrels create a beautiful woven pattern. Local artists display their vibrant wares along the walls, several tables surround the green tasting bar, and there's plenty of room outside beneath their bright red sail.

Visitors can choose from a wide variety of unique cheeses as an accompaniment to a favorite cider.

POSSIBILITIES

Hard Cider
Pomander
Whippersnapper
Orchard Brut
Rose
Minty
Ballyhoo
Pinch
Luck
Hornswaggle
Kingston Black
Wild Harvest

TASTINGS	TAKE HOME	RESERVATIONS
4 for $9	Cans: 4 for $8-$10	Walk in

VISIT

311 Fuller Ave. NE · Grand Rapids 49503

616.288.6904 · puxcider.com

Open year-round

Red Top Winery

BARODA · EST. 2017

Visitors to Red Top Winery will enjoy the expansive red bar that dominates the tasting room, with plenty of room for you and all your friends. Reservations for groups are not required, but they do have a 15-person group limit. The spaciousness continues with a large covered patio in the back and a lawn that runs right up to the vineyard surrounding the property. A new patio stretches out from the building, with plenty of seating areas dotting the lawn beyond.

Saturday afternoons brings live music in the summer and fall, and visitors are welcome to bring a picnic and relax in the sun.

POSSIBILITIES

Red/Rosé
Le Vin
Malbec
Syrah
Top Wire
Radiant Red
Rock 'N Red

White
Rum Barrel White
Caribbean Twist
El Vino
Pinot Grigio
MI Happy Wine
Lake Effect

Sparkling Cider
Hollerpeno
Raspberry Cherry
Turtle
Cucumber Basil

TASTINGS	TAKE HOME	RESERVATIONS
$12 per person	$13–$39	Walk in

VISIT

482 E. Snow Rd. • Baroda, MI 49101

269.473.2711 • info@redtopwinery.com • redtopwinery.com

Open year-round

Robinette's Apple Haus and Winery

GRAND RAPIDS · EST. 2006

If you love autumn, then a visit to Robinette's should definitely be in your plans. But you don't have to wait until the leaves start to fall to experience everything it has to offer. There's something here for everyone, from the fresh baked goods and warm donuts, to ice cream, and of course the wine.

The tasting room is housed in the cellar of the large barn to the right of the Apple Haus. Enter through a gift shop, turn right, and you're at the tasting bar. The barn is over 100 years old, and the rough stone walls and bark-covered timbers above provide an historical footnote to the wines on display throughout. The tasting bar fits several visitors comfortably. If you're looking for a quiet, relaxing visit, come on a weekday. Autumn weekends are fun, but hectic. Hayrides, corn maze, petting zoo, pumpkins, all the tasty treats — they all combine to create an irresistible attraction for hundreds of people. But sometimes that's part of the fun, isn't it?

POSSIBILITIES

Red/Rosé
Robin Red
Rapids Red

White
Robin White
White Gold
Harbor

Hard Cider
Barzilla's Cider
Orange Ginger
Heirloom
Rose
Hopped
Apple Cherry
Bill's Special Cider

TASTINGS
5 for $8

TAKE HOME
Bottles: $10–$14

RESERVATIONS
Walk in

VISIT
3142 4 Mile Rd. NE • Grand Rapids, MI 49525
616.361.7180 • contact through website • robinettes.com
Open year-round

Round Barn Estate

BARODA · EST. 1997

As its name suggests, Round Barn Estate is more than just a winery. Visitors can enjoy a tasting in the famous round barn, the beer barn, or outside at one of the seating areas scattered around their expansive lawn. Every weekend, live music brings guests who cart in their own lawn chairs, choose some tasty items from the food court, and settle in for a relaxing afternoon in the shade sipping on their favorite beverage. It might be wine, beer, or spirits; Round Barn Estate also includes a brewery and distillery.

Those who want to burn off some calories can hike the 3.5 mile trail between Round Barn and Tabor Hill Winery. Running through forest and vineyard, the trail is a unique way to explore the area. One thing you definitely need to explore before leaving the estate is the barn itself. Although it isn't always possible to go to the upper level, if it's open when you visit, stop in. Built in 1912 by Amish craftsmen in Indiana, it was moved in the 1990s and now provides the centerpiece and namesake for the estate.

POSSIBILITIES

Red/Rosé
Vineyard Rosé
Pinot Noir
Merlot LMS
Vineyard Red
Cabernet Sauvignon

White
Vineyard Tears
Sauvignon Blanc
Chardonnay LMS
Gewürztraminer

Fruit
Cran-Apple
Cranberry
Plum

Sparkling/Specialty
Artesia Spumante
Red Sangria
White Sangria
Crantini

TASTINGS	TAKE HOME	RESERVATIONS
3 for $12	$14–$33	Groups of 10 or more

VISIT

10983 Hills Rd. · Baroda, MI 49101

269.422.1617 · hello@roundbarn.com · roundbarn.com

Open year-round

The Sangria Shop

PORTAGE · EST. 2012

If you are looking for something out of the ordinary, The Sangria Shop in Portage will fit the bill. The Puerto Rican influence can't be missed with their focus on island traditions and recipes that have been passed down through the family. They also have expanded into distilling, with flavored vodka and rum.

The tasting room has plenty of space for friends to gather and enjoy their unique offerings.

POSSIBILITIES

Sangria
Classica
Tropical
Wildberry
Peachy Breeze
Ambrosia
Fragum
Tamarind
Passion Fruit

Spirits
Don Fernando Lime Vodka
Don Fernando Coconut Rum
Don Fernando Orange Vodka

TASTINGS	TAKE HOME	RESERVATIONS
5 for $8	Sangria $15 to $16	Walk in
	Spirits $25 to $30	

VISIT

8842 Portage Rd. • Portage, MI 49002

269.532.1629 • sangria.taina@gmail.com • thesangriashop.com

Open year-round

Sawyers Brewing Co.

MONTAGUE · EST. 2021

Generosity of spirit is alive and well at Sawyers Brewing Co., where they have celebrated the hands-on aspects of brewing and winemaking, and invite their visitors to join them. Classes are offered in wine, beer, and even cheese-making. The tasting room is the proof of their dedication to craft; they serve something for everyone, from beer and wine to their homemade cheeses.

The long bar provides plenty of room for visitors, and there are tables both inside and out for friends to linger over a favorite drink. On the weekends, live music and food trucks add to the festivities.

POSSIBILITIES

Hard Cider
Eezy Peezy Lemon Squeezy
Peaches O'Houlihan
Blackberry Bounce
Cherry Tart
Blood Orange

Wine
Muscato
Riesling
Cabernet Sauvignon

TASTINGS	TAKE HOME	RESERVATIONS
5 for $8	4 for $15	Walk in

VISIT

4574 Dowling St. • Montague, MI 49437

231.923.1986 • contact through website • sawyersbrewing.com

Open year-round

Speciation Cellars

GRAND RAPIDS · EST. 2016

Hidden behind the buildings that front Wealthy Street, Speciation Cellars attracts those who are open to new taste experiences and unique brewing methods. When visitors enter the gray, unassuming building, they are greeted with a wild mural over the bar, which highlights the antediluvian seas awash over Michigan eons ago. Depending on the day, you may be treated to a round of trivia, or invited to bring your own LPs to Vinyl Night.

There is a long bar and several tables inside, and an outdoor seating area—dogs are welcome—bordered by planters spilling over with colorful annuals. Enjoy a game of cornhole, or just sit and soak in this urban oasis. Although Speciation Cellars doesn't offer food, they welcome visitors to bring their own, and several restaurants within walking distance make a perfect place for take out.

POSSIBILITIES
Red/Rosé
Embers
Swim to the Moon
Marrow of the Spirit
Anoxia
Forgotten Lands
White
Animal Noises
Sparkling
The Gnashing
The Iron Bell
March to the Sea
Fruit/Cider
Deeper than Sky
Astral Dominion

TASTINGS	TAKE HOME	RESERVATIONS
A la carte	$15–$24	Walk in

VISIT

928 Wealthy St. SE · Grand Rapids, MI 49506

contact through website · speciationartisanales.com

Open year-round

St. Julian Winery

PAW PAW · EST. 1921

For over 100 years, St. Julian has held the title of Michigan's premiere winery, for good reason. They've been at their current location for nearly 90 years, and have built the business into the giant it is today. Tours are available at their main building in Paw Paw, where you can get an inkling of just how large this operation is.

With dozens of offerings in their tasting room, choosing will definitely take a bit of time. They also offer cheese trays as an accompaniment. They have plenty of room for groups, and a patio out front for visitors to enjoy the sunshine.

St. Julian Winery also has tasting rooms in Dundee (700 Freedom Ct.), Frankenmuth (127 S. Main St.), Metro Detroit (518 W. 14 Mile Rd, Troy), Rockford (4425 14 Mile Rd. NE), and Union Pier (9145 Union Pier Rd.).

POSSIBILITIES

Red/Rosé
Cabernet Franc
Cabernet Sauvignon
Holidaze
Red Heron
Frankemuth Rosé
Cap Drain #2

White
Albarino
Grüner Veltliner
Simply White
Blue Heron
Michcato
Marsanne

Sparkling
Dry Bubbly Rosé
Brut Champagne
Sweet Nancie
Sparkling Michcato
Sweet Nancie Raspberry
Sweet Nancie Cherry

Fruit
Cherry
Blueberry
Cranberry
Blackberry

Dessert
Moo-Low
Mint Moo-Low
Catherman's Port
Cream D'Or
Solera Cream Sherry
Vidal Blanc Ice Wine

TASTINGS	TAKE HOME	RESERVATIONS
6 for $8	$8–$35	For more than 8

VISIT

716 Kalamazoo St. • Paw Paw, MI 49079

800.732.6002 • wines@stjulian.com • stjulian.com

Open year-round

Stoney Ridge Vineyards

KENT CITY · EST. 2012

The red tasting room for Stoney Ridge Vineyards is perched on a hill overlooking a beautiful view that stretches for miles. Farmland and forests brush up against the vineyards extending from the lush lawn, and Adirondack chairs are an invitation to watch the summer clouds roll by. Inside, visitors have their choice of the large granite-topped bar or the cozy tables scattered throughout the spacious room. Outdoors, a covered patio—off-limits to pets—offers shaded views, and sunny sitting areas dot the lawn.

You'll be tempted to linger here, not only for the view, but they also have live music during the summer months, and a full kitchen with everything from soup, sandwiches, and wood-fired pizza to beautiful charcuterie boards. Reservations are recommended, and groups of more than eight visitors will need to make special accommodations.

POSSIBILITIES
Red/Rosé
Alice
Frick & Frack
Marquette
Stoney Ridge Red
Walk Thru Red
Marquette Rosé
White
Chardonnay
Inclinations
La Crescent
Swallow Barn White
Stoney Ridge White
Pinot Gris
Riesling
Crescent Moon
Itasca

TASTINGS	TAKE HOME	RESERVATIONS
5 for $10	$15–$22	For more than 8

VISIT

2255 Indian Lakes Rd. • Kent City, MI 49330

616.498.5468 • contact through website • stoneyridgevineyards.com

Open year-round

Tabor Hill Winery

BUCHANAN · EST. 1968

Resting on a slight rise, Tabor Hill Winery and Restaurant sits in the dappled shade of hardwoods, nestled amongst the vineyards. Their restaurant offers beautiful views of the vineyards, as well as a popular gourmet menu. Visitors can order pre-selected flights at the bar, or take a seat on the large deck outside. Stairs lead down to the patio and vineyard below, where cabanas are set up on the lawn. These shaded seating areas can be rented out in two-hour increments for groups of up to 8 guests. If you'd like a closer look at the property, you can have a "Tour and Taste" for $20, or choose their "Trolley Experience," which is a look at the production at both Tabor Hill and Round Barn Winery nearby. In fact, the Mt. Tabor Trail provides visitors the opportunity to hike from one winery to the other, winding through both vineyards and the shaded woods surrounding them.

Many activities at Tabor Hill require reservations, so it's best to plan ahead for your visit.

Tabor Hill also has a tasting room in Bridgman (10243 Red Arrow Hwy).

POSSIBILITIES
Red/Rosé
Rosé
Pinot Noir
Merlot
Syrah
Cabernet Sauvignon
White
Sauvignon Blanc
Pinot Griglo
Chardonnay
Dry Gewürztraminer
Pinot Blanc
Valvin Muscat
Riesling
Fruit
Farm Market Blueberry
Cherry
Sparkling
Grand Mark
Brut
Sparkling Demi-Sec

TASTINGS	TAKE HOME	RESERVATIONS
$12	$13–$50	For groups of 10 or more

VISIT
185 Mt. Tabor Rd. • Buchanan, MI 49107

269.422.1161 • hello@taborhill.com • taborhill.com

Open year-round

Tanglewood Winery

HOLLAND · EST. 2016

Down a gravel drive and nestled up to the surrounding pines is the smokey blue tasting room of Tanglewood Winery. The rustic setting is echoed in its interior, with wood-burned barrel tables and barnwood siding surrounding the bar. There is plenty of space for visitors both indoors and out, with two sitting areas outside offering views of the vineyard and the trees beyond.

Reservations are recommended for larger groups.

POSSIBILITIES

Red
Frontenac

White
Traminette

Fruit/Dessert
Blue Blood
Blue Silk
Beach Bum Blueberry
Apple Pie
Sweet Summer Sangria

TASTINGS	TAKE HOME	RESERVATIONS
Flight for $7	$15–$25	Walk in

VISIT

15811 Riley St. • Holland, MI 49424

616.375.9648 • contact through website • tanglewoodwinery.com

Open seasonally

Tempo Vino Winery

KALAMAZOO · EST. 2010

Downtown Kalamazoo has an eclectic mix of businesses that attract visitors from all over the area, which makes it a perfect location for Tempo Vino Winery. While many wineries are sought out for their pure Michigan ingredients, the vintners at Tempo Vino are unapologetically international. The ingredients used to create their wines come from California, Europe, and even Australia. And they want their visitors to have a hand in the creative process as well, offering the opportunity to craft your own batch of wine according to your personal taste.

The tasting room is narrow, with a tall ceiling, exposed brick on the walls, and large front windows facing the street. Visitors should call ahead as their hours may change due to private parties throughout the week.

POSSIBILITIES

Red/Rosé
Twilight Time
I've Got a Gal in Kalamazoo House Red
Libertango Malbec
Alla Terra Barolo
Alex's Amore Amarone
Moonlight Serenade Cabernet Sauvignon

White
Green Eyes Pinot Grigio
Walwood Hall Sauvignon Blanc
I've Got a Gal in Kalamazoo House White
Chattanooga Choo-Choo Chardonnay
Ramona Palace Riesling

Fruit/Dessert
Peach Chardonnay
Strawberry Blush
Black Raspberry Merlot
Wildberry Shiraz

TASTINGS	TAKE HOME	RESERVATIONS
5 for $8	$13–$25	Walk in

VISIT

260 E. Michigan Ave. • Kalamazoo, MI 49007

269.342.9463 • tempovinowinery@gmail.com • tempovinowinery.com

Open year-round

Twine Urban Winery

KALAMAZOO · EST. 2019

If you are looking for a break from the hectic pace of city life, and want to relax in a friendly and welcoming atmosphere, then Twine is for you. The dark floors and bright chandeliers combine to create a modern interior, and there's even a colorful space devoted to selfies for a bit of fun. There are several tables near the tasting bar, and an outdoor patio for sunny afternoons.

Offerings include a charcuterie board, dip, and wine cocktails. This winery is cashless.

POSSIBILITIES

Red/Rosé
Briarwood
Bubbling Rosé
Cabenet Franc
Cabernet Sauvignon
Capriccio
French Bordeaux
Malbec
Meritage
Roche Black

White
Chardonnay
Roche Blanc
Sweet Riesling

Fruit/Sparkling
Green Apple Sangria
Peach Mango
Pineapple Pear
Pomegranate

TASTINGS	TAKE HOME	RESERVATIONS
6 for $15	$12–$28	Recommended

VISIT

1319 Portage St. • Kalamazoo, MI 49001

269.270.3278 • contact through website • therochecollection.com

Open year-round

Vander Mill Ciders

GRAND RAPIDS · EST. 2006

Vander Mill Ciders' tasting room, in downtown Grand Rapids, offers visitors a relaxing place have a meal, enjoy some cider, and wind down with friends after a hectic day. There's plenty of room at the long bar, and the large space is filled with tables for drinking and dining, along with windows that overlook the production floor. They offer great food, but you have to order from the window at the end of the room. Smash burgers and wings are the perfect accompaniment to the large variety of ciders on tap. Or treat yourself to tabletop S'Mores, toasting marshmallows yourself right at the table.

Outside, picnic tables dot the landscaped front yard; choose a sunny spot in the center or walk down the sloping yard to a pair of Adirondacks beneath the cherry trees. They also offer up live music and open mic nights on occasion, but the centerpiece on their calendar has got to be the professional wrestling events they hold on the floor of the production room!

POSSIBILITIES
Hard Cider
Vandy
Hard Apple
Totally Roasted
Brut
Rosé
Puff
Ginger Zero
BLUish Gold
Apple Raspberry
Ninuca Pine
Cherry Chuckle
Cyser Van Doom
Green Mill
Besieged
Bou Chrétién
Chapman's Blend
Chapman's Oaked
Too Gold

TASTINGS	TAKE HOME	RESERVATIONS
4 for $12	4 pack $8 to $9	Walk in
	Bottles $9	

VISIT

505 Ball Ave. NE • Grand Rapids, MI 49503

616.259.8828 • cider@vandermill.com • vandermill.com

Open year-round

Vineyard 2121

BENTON HARBOR · EST. 2015

Follow the gravel drive past a row of hardwoods and up a small rise, and the red tasting room of Vineyard 2121 is waiting for you. Its beautiful circular tasting bar has plenty of seats, and there are tables scattered throughout the spacious interior. Outside, a covered deck provides the perfect place to settle in with your favorite wine and look out over the vineyards and forest beyond.

Live music is a staple every weekend in the summer and early fall. Charcuterie boards are available, as well as soups, sandwiches, and mac and cheese. Visitors will also enjoy the delectable weekend dinner specials, from smothered pork chops to jambalaya and everything in between. With all this waiting for you, it really does become a special destination.

POSSIBILITIES

Red/Rosé
Chambourcin
Third Time's a Charm
Miss Fortune
Merlot
Cabernet Franc
Cabernet Sauvignon
De Chaunac Prés Du Lac
Chambourcin Rosé

White
Chardonnay
Seyval Blanc
Polite Disillusionment
Sparkling Michigan Bubbly
Riesling
Vineyard 2121 Blush
Vineyard 2121 White

Ciders
Pappy's Hard Ciders
Limited Edition Ciders

TASTINGS	TAKE HOME	RESERVATIONS
4 for $15	$17–$39	For 8 or more

VISIT

4110 Red Arrow Hwy • Benton Harbor, MI 49022

269.849.0109 • deb@vineyard2121.com • vineyard2121.com

Open year-round

73

Virtue Cider

FENNVILLE · EST. 2011

If you thirst for the country life, as well as a good cider, head to Virtue Cider in Fennville. Visitors are welcome to explore the grounds, following trails which lead to a variety of farm animals in pens; farm tours are available to reserve through their website. Pigs, chickens, goats and sheep are scattered about the property, and enclosures are moved on occasion to help with the agricultural needs of the farm. Lawn games, hammocks, and beautiful plantings surround the timber-framed tasting room.

Inside, the bar can get a bit crowded, especially on weekends, but there is so much outside seating, beneath a covered pavilion, or at picnic tables across the lawn, that there is plenty of room to spread out. Stop by and enjoy a game of horseshoes and discover your favorite cider.

POSSIBILITIES

Hard Ciders
Brut
Old Spot
Percheron
The Mitten
Cherry Mitten
Maple Mitten
Michigan Apple
Michigan Cherry
Those Women from Michigan
Hot Spiced Hard Cider
Rosalita
Salut!
Cardinale
Lapinette
Rosé
Pear

TASTINGS	TAKE HOME	RESERVATIONS
6 for $18	6 cans/$10	Walk in

VISIT
2170 62nd St. · Fennville, MI 49408
269.722.3232 · contact through website · virtuecider.com
Open year-round

Warner Vineyards

PAW PAW · EST. 1938

There isn't a cuter spot in the city of Paw Paw than on the banks of its namesake river, where you'll find the tasting room of Warner Vineyards. Its interesting architecture is due to its proximity to this water source, as it was originally the waterworks station for the town; the brick building was built in 1898. A small bridge leads visitors from the parking area to the brick walkway surrounding the building. Inside, the beautiful tasting bar has plenty of room, and there are additional tables beneath brick arches.

Outside, the river is on display, with large decks along its banks, creating the perfect spot to savor the tastes and sounds of nature. An outdoor amphitheater provides a stage for weekend music, and with the addition of the Warner Brew Haus in 2021, visitors with various tastes will find something they enjoy here.

Warner Vineyards also has tasting rooms in Holland (26 E. 8th St.), Marshall (116 E. Michigan Ave.), and South Haven (515 Williams St.).

TASTINGS	TAKE HOME	RESERVATIONS
5 for $8	$13–$40	For groups of 7 or more

VISIT

706 S. Kalamazoo St. · Paw Paw, MI 49079

269.657.3165 · hello@warnerwines.com · warnerwines.com

Open year-round

POSSIBILITIES

Red/Rosé
Veritas
S.O.S.
Ruby Red
Pinot Noir
Merlot
Mello Red
Cabernet Sauvignon
Cabernet Franc
2Cab/Merlot Dry Red
Classic Blush
Dry Rosé

White
Grapes of Love
Riesling
Chardonnay Reserve
Sauvignon Blanc
Classic White Demi-Sec
Pinot Grigio
Gewürztraminer

Fruit
Blueberry Splash
Holiberry
Peach & Honey
Red Currant
Sangria

Cider
Caboozy Lil' Cherry
Caboozy Lil' Crisp Hard Apple

Specialty
Port
Solera Cream Sherry
Sparkling Riesling
Vidal Blanc Ice Wine

White Pine Winery and Vineyards

ST. JOSEPH · EST. 2010

Nestled in a cozy downtown storefront, the White Pine Winery tasting room offers guests a quiet interlude to sample a few of their award-winning wines. High top tables are set up amidst a cute boutique gift shop, and the pressed-tin ceiling tiles and exposed brick walls bring a sense of history to the tasting room.

Silver Beach is just a few blocks away, and a wine tasting is the perfect ending to a day in the sun.

POSSIBILITIES

Red/Rosé
Reserve Merlot
Reserve Serendipity
Reserve Borealis
Dune Shadow Red
Red Expression

White
Traminette
Reserve Riesling
Dry Riesling
Pinot Grigio
White Expression

Dessert
Ice Wine

TASTINGS
4 for $8

TAKE HOME
$11–$35

RESERVATIONS
For groups of 7 or more

VISIT
317 State St. • St. Joseph, MI 49085
269.281.0098 • contact through website • whitepinewinery.com
Open year-round

The Winery at Young Farms

MECOSTA · EST. 2017

Beautiful hardwoods shade the parking area and red barn beyond, and the flatness of the land in this area emphasizes the endless sky above. This land has been farmed for well over 100 years, and its current incarnation has incorporated a vineyard into the mix, resulting in The Winery at Young Farms. One of the barns on the property has been converted, and its large arched door leads to an inviting country chic tasting room. Outside, there's a seating area along the covered front porch, as well as a sunnier spot along the side, with plenty of room to sit a spell and enjoy the relaxing countryside, or explore the vineyard just yards away. Thursdays provide a chance to catch some live music, and the Friday night dessert and wine offerings are popular. Young Farms also hosts a Words & Wine bookclub, which sounds perfect.

POSSIBILITIES

Red/Rosé
Eugene's Red
Father Tom's Red
Herb's Red

White
Flossie's White
Diane's White
Sonny's White

Fruit
Bertha's Blue
Big Boy Brosé

Cider
Them Apples
Hippity Hoppity
Herbal Remedy
Babymaker
Sweet Cinner

TASTINGS	TAKE HOME	RESERVATIONS
5 for $5	$10–$22	For groups of 10 or more

VISIT

8396 70th Ave. • Mecosta, MI 49332 • 989.506.5142

markandabby@thewineryatyoungfarms.com • thewineryatyoungfarms.com

Open seasonally

Distilleries of Southwest Michigan

Bier Distillery
5295 West River Drive NE, Comstock Park, MI 49321
616.888.9746
Whiskey, Rye Whiskey, Bourbon, Brandy,
Gin, Rum, Vodka, Absinthe, Moonshine

Burl & Sprig
500 W. Western Ave, Muskegon, MI 49440
231.900.1313
Rum, Vodka, Gin

Coppercraft Distillery
184 120th, Holland, MI 49424 and
tasting room in Saugatuck
616.796.8274
Bourbon, Rye Whiskey, Vodka, Applejack, Gin, Rum

Corey Lake Distillery
(Hubbard's Corey Lake Orchard)
12147 Corey Lake Rd., Three Rivers, MI 49093
269.244.5690
Brandy

Eastern Kille Distillery
700 Ottawa Ave NW, Grand Rapids, MI 49503
616.893.3305
Bourbon, Gin, Rye Whiskey, Coffee Liqueur

Green Door Distilling
429 E. North St., Kalamazoo, MI 49007
269.205.3398
Gin, Bourbon, Whiskey

Gull Lake Distilling Company
92 E. Michigan Ave., Galesburg, MI 49053
269.200.5329
Vodka, Gin, Rum, Moonshine

Iron Shoe Distillery
3 North 3rd St., Niles, MI 49120
269.262.0454
Vodka, Rum, Limoncello, Orangecello,
Whiskey, Crème Liqueur

Kalamazoo Stillhouse
618 E. Michigan Ave., Kalamazoo, MI 49007
206.376.0937
Whiskey, Gin, Vodka, Rum

Long Road Distillers
537 Leonard St. NW, Grand Rapids, MI 49504
(tasting rooms in Charlevoix and Grand Haven)
616.228.4924
Vodka, Gin, Aquavit, Whiskey, Bourbon,
Brandy, Rum, Liqueurs

Michigan Moonshine Distillery
4005 Chicago Dr. SW, Grandville, MI 49418
616.259.1000
Moonshine, Rum

New Holland Spirits
201 Culver St., Saugatuck, MI 49453
616.294.3436
Bourbon, Gin, Vodka, Rum, Whiskey, Liqueur

Round Barn Distillery (on the Round Barn Estate)
10983 Hills Rd., Baroda, MI 49101
269.422.1617
Vodka, Rum, Agave, Whiskey, Bourbon, Gin

Thornapple Artisan Spirits
(part of Thornapple Brewing)
6262 28th St. SE, Grand Rapids, MI 49546
616.288.6907
Moonshine, Whiskey, Bourbon, Rum,
Gin, Vodka, Agave Spirit

Wise Men Distillery
4717 Broadmoor Ave. SE Suite F,
Grand Rapids, MI 49512
616.805.7003
Bourbon, Vodka, Whiskey, Gin, Moonshine, Rum

Wonderland Distilling Co.
1989 Lakeshore Dr., Muskegon, MI 49441
231.788.9777
Whiskey, Vodka, Gin

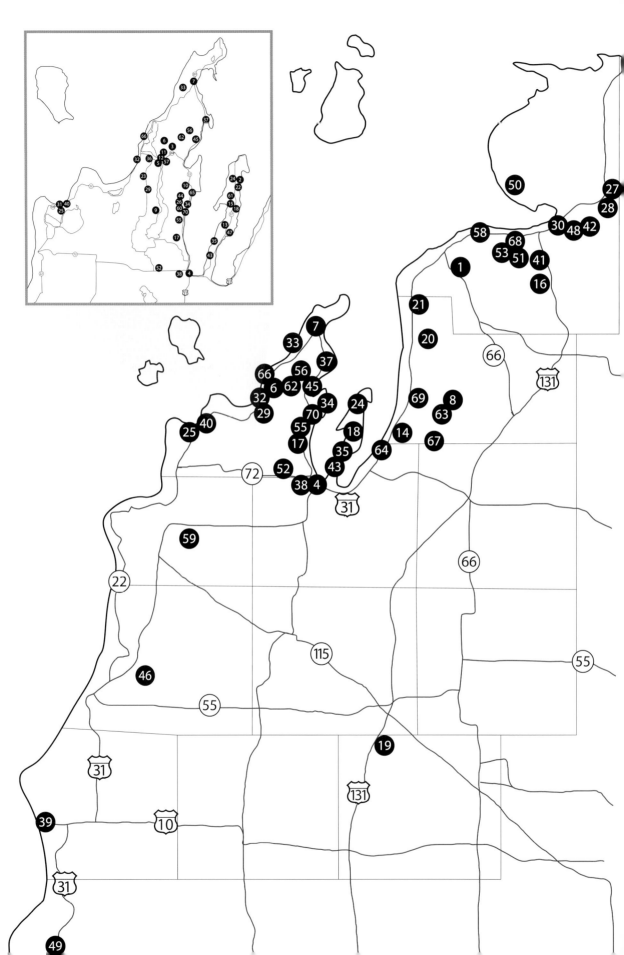

Northwest Michigan

2 Lads Winery

TRAVERSE CITY · EST. 2008

Driving up the curving path to 2 Lads Winery, vineyards lace the hillside, and the modern lines of the tasting room provide an interesting parallel to the nature surrounding it. A façade of corrugated metal, floor-to-ceiling windows, and stone pillars framing the entryway all combine to create a strong, yet beautiful building.

The modern aesthetic holds true throughout the interior as well. But inside, the view is everything. The wall of windows which dominates the exterior now looks over gently sloping fields and across East Grand Traverse Bay. The view goes on forever, and empties your mind of all the stresses of the everyday.

A small gift shop opens up beyond the bar and private tastings are given in rooms nearby. Private tastings are $35, and these run about an hour. If you want to know even more about the day-to-day operations, private tours are available for $50 per person. Both the private tastings and tours require reservations. Motor coaches and RVs over 25 ft. are not allowed.

POSSIBILITIES

Red
Pinot Noir
Pinot Noir Cuvée Beatrice
Pinot Noir D. Cuvée
Cabernet Franc/Merlot
Cabernet Franc Reserve
Rola Red

White
Pinot Grigio
Chardonnay
Reserve Chardonnay
Riesling – 2L Vineyard
Riesling – Fouch Vineyard
Late Harvest Riesling
Rosé

Sparkling
Pinot Grigio
Crisp

TASTINGS	TAKE HOME	RESERVATIONS
5 for $12	$17–$75	For groups of 6 or more

VISIT

16985 Smokey Hollow Rd. • Traverse City, MI 49686

231.223.7722 • info@2lwinery • 2lwinery.com

Open year-round

45 North Vineyard and Winery

LAKE LEELANAU · EST. 2006

From the peak of its red-roofed cupola to the weathered gray siding, the tasting room of Forty-Five North is filled with charm. Inside, the post-and-beam construction draws the eyes upward to its pitched roof, affording an open and inviting tasting experience. There is something for everyone here, from reds, whites, and rosés, to fruit, cider, and dessert wines. They offer a charcuterie plate, as well as a few other smalls. Once you choose your favorite, take a glass outside and relax on their shady deck, or take in a game of bocce ball on the front lawn. It's like visiting with an old friend.

In the summer months, group tours are offered every Saturday at noon for $20. Lasting about an hour, the tour will take you through the fields and production facility, and give you a glimpse into the history of the winery. Reservations are recommended.

POSSIBILITIES

Red and Rosé
Pinot Noir Rosé
Rosé
Fandango #18
Pinot Noir
45 Red
Lemberger

White
Reserve Chardonnay
Dry Riesling
Unwooded Chardonnay
Sauvignon Blanc
Marsanne
Pinot Gris
Reserve Pinot Gris
Reserve Rieesling
45 White

Specialty
Sparkling Peach
Sparkling Strawberry

TASTINGS	TAKE HOME	RESERVATIONS
5 for $7	$17–$36	For groups of 10 or more

VISIT

8580 E. Horn Rd. • Lake Leelanau, MI 49653 • 231.271.1188

info@fortyfivenorth.com • fortyfivenorth.com

Open year-round

1918 Cellars

CHARLEVOIX · EST. 2018

Many Michiganders know of Castle Farms; in the 70s, it was a place to rock out with your favorite bands, and today it has become a mecca for those who want to be married in grand style. Visitors can admire the gardens, fountains and ponds, as well as the beautiful stone architecture. But there is the added attraction of the estate's own winery: 1918 Cellars.

Take a path through the butterfly garden, follow the paving stones and emerge near the entrance to the tasting room, which is housed in one of the corner towers near the Queen's Courtyard. Inside, the stone walls and wooden rib structure supporting the roof give it a medieval flair, and it's a peaceful place to enjoy a lunch while sampling their wines.

POSSIBILITIES

Red/Rosé
Reflection
Rosé
Pinot Noir
Stonemason
Serenity Red

White
Visionary
Sauvignon Blanc
Chardonnay
Birch Lake White
Riesling
Pinot Grigio

TASTINGS	TAKE HOME	RESERVATIONS
5 for $7	$19–$33	Walk in

VISIT

5052 M-66 • Charlevoix, MI 49720

231.237.0884 • info@castlefarms.com • castlefarms.com

Open year-round

Acoustic Meads

TRAVERSE CITY · EST. 2006

Whe you step inside the taproom of Acoustic Meads, you are instantly welcomed, whole heartedly. You are now part of their inclusive community, and they definitely want you to relax and have a great time. Board games, a piano, steel drum, flights served in guitars—the vibe is young, and very accepting. Although the tasting room is small, there is a bar and several tables for visitors. Outdoors, the front patio offers comfortable seating at umbrella-shaded tables. They have a few snacks, but you are welcome to bring in food from the several nearby restaurants. Live music is a natural fit at this establishment; check their website for scheduled performers.

POSSIBILITIES

Meads
BluezBeri
Cherry Bzzz
Honey Bzzz
Calypso
Strawberi Rosé
Hip Hop
Jazzberi
Hard Cider
Rock Hard
Rock Steady
Punk
Cyser
Soul
Lovely Rita
Velvet Elvis

TASTINGS	TAKE HOME	RESERVATIONS
2 oz. for $2	Cans: $5–$7	Walk in

VISIT

119 N. Maple St. • Traverse City, MI

231.714.5028 • contact through website • drinkacoustic.com

Open year-round

Amoritas Vineyards

LAKE LEELANAU · EST. 2015

The tasting room for Amoritas Vineyards is small but welcoming, with a short bar for tastings and a comfy lounging area for a longer visit. When you have time to sit a spell, outdoor seating on the front porch is like visiting your neighbor. There is a private tasting room for groups who may need a bit more room, and a private vineyard tour is also offered. Both require reservations.

POSSIBILITIES

Red
Points North

White
Pinot Blanc
Pinot Gris
Happenstance
Chardonnay
Dry Riesling
Mary's Folly White Field Blend
Mary's Folly White Carbonated
Hail Mary Sweet Riesling
Semi-Dry Riesling
Fascinatorz

Fruit
Pit Stop (Cherry)

TASTINGS	TAKE HOME	RESERVATIONS
5 for $7	$18–$23	Walk in

VISIT

6701 E. Duck Lake Rd. · Lake Leenanau, MI 49653

231.994.2300 · info@amoritasvineyards.com · amoritasvineyards.com

Open year-round

Aurora Cellars

LAKE LEELANAU · EST. 2015

The Aurora Cellars tasting room, a lovely Italian-style farmhouse, is tucked into a wide expanse of rolling hills bordered by strips of forest. A lavender-lined path welcomes visitors, and once inside they'll appreciate the mellow lighting and relaxing atmosphere. Outdoor areas provide plenty of space to enjoy the green fields and wide-open skies, and the beautiful location is a popular wedding venue as well.

POSSIBILITIES

Red and Rosé
Rosé
Radiance
Pinot Noir
Blaufränkisch
Rosso
Cabernet Franc

White
Pinot Grigio
Sauvignon Blanc
Barrel Fermented Chardonnay
Luminous

Sparkling
Blanc de Noirs
Brut
Brut Rosé

Cider
Heirloom
Seasonal

TASTINGS	TAKE HOME	RESERVATIONS
5 for $7	$18–$38	For more than 8

VISIT

7788 E. Horn Rd. • Lake Leelanau, MI 49653

231.403.0593 • contact through website • auroracellars.com

Open year-round

Baia Estate

NORTHPORT · EST. 2016

The tasting room for Baia Estate has recently moved from the New Bohemian Café to the Northport Union, an event space directly across the street from the café. While the dinners and other events at the Union feature Baia wines, if you are interested in dropping by for just a tasting, definitely call first to check out your options.

POSSIBILITIES

Red/ Rosé
Pinot Noir
Rosé

White
Pinot Grigio
Chardonnay
Riesling

Sparkling
Bubbs
Rosécco
Lambo

TASTINGS	TAKE HOME	RESERVATIONS
$2 each	$20–$22	Call First

VISIT

107 Nagonaba St. • Northport, MI 49670

231.386.2461 • eric@thenorthportunion.com • baiaestate.com

Open year-round

Bee Well Meadery

BELLAIRE · EST. 2014

The tiny town of Bellaire has a secret: it's home to one of the best meaderies in northern Michigan. Housed in a gabled storefront, complete with weathered siding, Bee Well Meadery has a friendly and welcoming ambiance. From the hexagon shelves to the bees burned into the bar top, this place is all about the honey. Their meads begin with locally-sourced honey, and they have plenty on tap for your pleasure.

The bar runs nearly the length of the room, and there are several other seating areas; they also offer non-alcoholic drinks and bar snacks.

POSSIBILITIES

Mead
Antrim Apple Pie
Ginger Peach
Cherry Vanilla
Sweet Melissa
Zest Love

Cider
Gin Blossom
Zoot Suit Riot
Killer Queen
The Ghost
Harrison
Kings Cherry
Comfortably Plum
White's Harvest
The North
Spy vs. Citra
The Krampus
Da Yoopers
Crabinette
The Wickson
The Heathen

TASTINGS	TAKE HOME	RESERVATIONS
$2–3 each	4-pack cans: $11–$12	Walk in

VISIT

116 N. Bridge St. • Bellaire, MI 49615 • 231.350.7116
info@beewellmeadery.com • beewellmeadery.com
Open year-round

Bel Lago Vineyards and Winery

CEDAR · EST. 1999

Asunny patio is a primary draw for many visitors, and Bel Lago has one of the prettiest. Surrounded by landscaped flower beds with a view of the blue waters of Lake Leelanau, the sitting area even boasts a relaxing waterfall. Shade is provided by umbrellas and a canopy, but if the weather is too chilly, embrace the view from the bank of windows inside. The tasting room offers a large bar and several tables surrounding it, and a window which looks over the production facility below. For those who like to pair their wine with a little something, they offer an interesting charcuterie pizza, as well as several others.

Live music is offered on Sundays, with special celebrations and charity events running throughout the year.

POSSIBILITIES

Red/Rosé
Pinot Noir
Bel Lago Red
Solia
Tempesta

White
Pinot Grigio & Chardonnay
Pinot Grigio
Chardonnay
Auxerrois Reserve
Auxerrois Stainless
Gewürztraminer
Soleil Blanc
Dry Riesling

Fruit/Sparkling
Raspberry Vera
Cherry
Cherry Dessert

Cider
Raspberry
Siegerrebe
Hopped
Slim Crickets

TASTINGS	TAKE HOME	RESERVATIONS
5 for $6	$14–$36	Walk in

VISIT

6530 S. Lake Shore Dr. • Cedar, MI 49621

231.228.4800 • bellagowinery@gmail.com • bellago.com

Open year-round

Black Star Farms

SUTTONS BAY · EST. 1998

Black Star Farms is one of the preeminent destinations for wine lovers across the Midwest, without a doubt. The tasting room is a beautiful open design, with a circular bar in the center and curved beams above. The soaring space gives room for a skylight far overhead. If this were the only thing to see here, it would be worth it. But there's so much more.

Across the drive from the tasting room, the Hearth and Vine Café offers farm-to-table treats that you can enjoy on its shaded patio. Grand Traverse Distillery is also on site, and the café offers cocktails using their own spirits.

Near the tasting room and café, the Black Star Inn offers the finishing touch, and visitors can spend their time on one of several porches at the inn or tasting room soaking up the sunshine in a beautiful northern Michigan setting.

Black Star Farms also has a tasting room on Old Mission Peninsula (360 McKinley Rd. E.)

POSSIBILITIES

Red/Rosé

A Capella Pinot Noir
Arcturos Pinot Noir
Select Pinot Noir
Red House Pinot Noir
Arcturos Gamay Noir
Nouveau Marquette
Arcturos Merlot
Vintners Select

White

Arcturos Pinot Gris
Arcturos Pinot Blanc
Arcturos Pinot Noir Blanc
Arcturos Grüner Veltliner
Arcturos Sauvignon Blanc
Arcturos Cur Lie Chardonnay
Arcturos Barrel Aged Chardonnay
Arcturos Gewürztraminer
Arcturos Dry Riesling
Tribute Off-Dry Riesling

TASTINGS	TAKE HOME	RESERVATIONS
5 for $7	$9–$54	Walk in

VISIT

10844 E. Revold Rd. · Suttons Bay, MI 49682 · 231.944.1270
clopez@blackstarfarms.com · blackstarfarms.com
Open year-round

Blustone Vineyards

LAKE LEELANAU · EST. 2005

The clean modern lines of Blustone's tasting room accentuate the natural world outside their expanse of windows, allowing no distraction to enjoying the beautiful views. The building is positioned at the top of a small hill, with a curve of forest encircling it from behind. Rows of vines run down gently sloping hills until they disappear in the distance. Inside, an angled bar provides plenty of room for visitors, and a large patio is a welcome outdoor space. Hydrangeas border the seating area, and there's a fire pit to ward off that northern chill.

POSSIBILITIES

Red/ Rosé
Winemaker's Red
Ad-Lib
Pinot Noir Rosé

White
Riesling
Pinot Grigio
Gewürztraminer
Naked Chardonnay
Latitude
Pinot Gris

Dessert/Sparkling
Late Harvest Riesling
Connexion
Blu Sparkling Riesling

Cider
Crisp Apple
Ginger Apple
Cranberry Apple

TASTINGS
5 for $8

TAKE HOME
$12–$34

RESERVATIONS
For groups larger than 6

VISIT
780 N. Sylt Rd. • Lake Leelanau, MI 49653
231.256.0146 • blustonevineyards.com
Open year-round

Boathouse Vineyards

LAKE LEELANAU · EST. 2009

Wouldn't it be fun to get in your boat for a relaxing cruise, and pull up at an award-winning winery along the water's edge? It's entirely possible at Boathouse Vineyards, whose barn-red tasting room is on the banks of the narrows joining north and south Lake Leelanau. From the dock, it's just a short walk up the gravel path to a row of Adirondack chairs, and the covered porch beyond. Of course, you could also approach by car and still have a great time watching the boats move slowly past. Bring some food and make a picnic of it. Live music is offered Wednesday and Saturday during the summer months. Inside, the horseshoe-shaped bar has plenty of room, and additional tables look out across the lawn.

POSSIBILITIES

Red/Rosé
Overboard
Rock the Boat
Pinot Noir
Pinot Noir Rosé
Boathouse Red
Merlot

White
Pinot Blanc
Unoaked Chardonnay
Pinot Grigio
Dry Dock Riesling
Knot Too Sweet Riesling
Boathouse Bubbly
Seas the Day
Muscat

Hard Cider/Fruit
Peach
Raspberry
Reel Cherry

TASTINGS
$1 each

TAKE HOME
$16–$32

RESERVATIONS
Walk in

VISIT

115 St. Mary's St., Lake Leelanau, MI 49653 • 231.256.7115
info@boathousevineyards.com • boathousevineyards.com
Open year-round

Bonobo Winery

TRAVERSE CITY · EST. 2014

Nestled amongst vineyards with views that extend to the lake, Bonobo is an inviting place to spend an afternoon. Its extensive layout offers plenty of room at the bar, and quiet seating areas filled with comfortable leather provide the perfect spot to catch up with friends. An outdoor patio looks out over Grand Traverse Bay, and offers the opportunity to catch a gorgeous sunset. Walk down the stairs to view the large Bonobo mural on the back wall, he looks very dapper in his pin-striped suit surveying his domain. The winery supports the work of the Bonobo Conservancy; ask how you can join them.

There are several opportunities for a special tasting. The reserved wine tasting is accompanied by a staff member and is $20 per person. The winery tour is $40 per person, while the crème de la crème would be the food and wine pairing at $50 per person. All require reservations. The dinner is only available on weekends, but they also offer an interesting assortment of small plates, from a charcuterie board to crab cakes and fried goat cheese.

POSSIBILITIES
Red/Rosé
Pinot Noir
BDX
Rosé
Bonobo Red
White
Pinot Gris
Riesling
Chardonnay

TASTINGS	TAKE HOME	RESERVATIONS
5 for $10	$22–$48	Walk in

VISIT
12011 Center Rd., Traverse City, MI 49686 • 231.282.9463
info@bonobowinery.com • bonobowinery.com
Open year-round

Bos Wine

ELK RAPIDS · EST. 2021

Combining the best of two worlds, the vintners at Bos Wine are working from their strengths: a past spent in California wine country, and a present in the heart of Michigan's. Their wines are a collection of ingredients from both regions, creating an opportunity to taste both side by side.

The old white farmhouse has an outdoor seating area in the backyard near a wild expanse of flowers, with an old red barn creating the perfect country backdrop. A curated wine tasting experience is available for $40. Reservations are strongly advised, as their tasting room is small and often reserved for private parties.

POSSIBILITIES

Red/Rosé
DEO
Ruby
Phoenix Ranch
Moon
Blaufränkisch Rosé

White
Wishflower
Amber
Riesling
Peridot

Sparkling
Methode Agricole

TASTINGS	TAKE HOME	RESERVATIONS
Reserved tasting: $28	$26–$48	Highly recommended

VISIT

135 Ames St., Elk Rapids, MI 49629 · 231.498.2073

info@boswine.com · boswine.com

Open year-round

Bowers Harbor Vineyards

TRAVERSE CITY · EST. 1991

A more welcoming entrance to a winery cannot be found. Bright plantings border the sidewalk. A shaded walkway, its pergola heavily covered in grape vines, leads visitors past vistas of vineyards with the lake in the distance. Peaceful seating arrangements are scattered throughout the yard, or larger groups can take a seat on their patio. A fire pit can ward off the chill of those northern fall days, and there is also a nature trail for those who would like to explore. Everything here encourages relaxation, even the vineyard dog who winds his way between the visitors, pausing for a good boy pat or scratch of the ears.

Bowers Harbor is the second-oldest winery on Old Mission Peninsula (the oldest is Chateau Grand Traverse) and they offer daily tours for those who want to get to know this friendly winery better. Reservations are required (48 hrs. prior is recommended) and the cost is $20. The also offer a longer tour and tasting for $40. Visiting in the winter? Tour the vineyard via snowshoes, which they will provide.

POSSIBILITIES
Red
Bowers Harbor Red
Pinot Noir, Nicholas
Pinot Noir, Wind Whistle
Claret, Wind Whistle
Shiraz, JBS Reserve
Proprietors' Reserve
White
Pinot Grigio
Unwooded Chardonnay, Big Paw
Chardonnay RLS Reserve
Riesling, Block II
Riesling, Smokey Hollow
Sparkling
Blanc de Blanc Cuvée Evan
Brut Rosé
Riesling, Stonehouse

TASTINGS	TAKE HOME	RESERVATIONS
5 for $5	$16–$55	Groups of 8 or more

VISIT
2896 Bowers Harbor Rd. • Traverse City, MI 49686
231.223.7615 • info@bowersharbor.com • bowersharbor.com
Open year-round

Boyne Valley Vineyards

PETOSKEY · EST. 2016

There is a relaxed and friendly vibe inside the tan barn at Boyne Valley. Weekends include live music, and a large tasting bar with numerous seating areas offer lots of space to spread out. They have a fire pit for those chilly evenings, and when the snow flies, consider this a great destination for snowshoe fun. One of the unique attractions is their tree house: an elevated deck encapsulating a grove of trees, which brings visitors closer to the canopy. Surround yourself with vineyards and the reds and golds of the forest during a sunny fall afternoon; you won't want to leave.

POSSIBILITIES

Red
Foxhole Red
Autumn Rosé
Hodge Podge
Short's Hill Red
Rosé
Pinot Noir
White
Cayuga White
Snow Cat White
La Crescent
Fruit
Red Raspberry

TASTINGS	TAKE HOME	RESERVATIONS
4 for $10	$18–$39	Walk in

VISIT

05325 U.S. 131 S. • Petoskey, MI 49770

231.373.2090 • boynevalleyvineyards.com

Open year-round

Brengman Brothers

TRAVERSE CITY · EST. 2010

Brengman Brothers, overlooking the west bay, brings the arts front and center, and has created the perfect canvas to display it. Inside, the soaring ceiling leaves the support beams exposed, and the stone fireplace with its floor to ceiling stonework dominates the seating area. A closer look reveals beautiful peacock tiles accenting the rough stone around it. The walls are decorated with artist's designs for the labels they've used, and they provide a gorgeous ribbon of color throughout. Artwork continues outdoors in the form of wine barrel and metal sculptures. Seating areas dot the wide lawn, which brushes against the vineyards sloping down the hill.

POSSIBILITIES

Red/Rosé
Pinot Noir Rosé
SauvFranc
Traverse Coast Rosé
Pinot Noir

White
Block 65 Blend
Riesling Trocken
Riesling Auslese
Riesling Dry

Sparkling
Two Long Cool Climate Fizz
Two Long Cool Climate Fizz Rosé
DaGudScht Blanc de Blancs

Dessert/Aromatized
Gewürztraminer SGN
Cherry Dessert Wine
Amaro
Sweet Vermouth
Dry Vermouth

TASTINGS	TAKE HOME	RESERVATIONS
$5–$15	$14–$55	Walk in

VISIT

9720 S. Center Highway • Traverse City, MI 49684

231.421.5611 • contact through website • brengmanbrothers.com

Open year-round

Brys Estate Vineyard & Winery

TRAVERSE CITY · EST. 2004

The beautiful tasting room of Brys Estate is a wonderful mix of bright red and white farm-style architecture on the outside, and a world of tradition inside. The bar itself is dark, and behind it, the brick wall ends with a gentle arch, showcasing the beautiful vaulted ceiling above. Both the brick and the vaulted wooden ceilings continue throughout the building.

If you would like to enjoy a tasting inside at one of the many wrought iron tables, or even in the barrel room itself, reservations are highly recommended. But walk-ins can nearly always find a seat at the expansive outdoor deck, which overlooks the vineyard and East Grand Traverse Bay in the distance.

Brys Estate offers something for every season of the year. The fall colors are gorgeous, spring blooms enliven us, and in summer, there is a beautiful 12-acre flower garden just down the hill from the tasting room, filled with beautiful plantings of lavender, coneflowers, cosmos, hydrangeas, lilies, and many other varieties.

POSSIBILITIES

Red/Rosé
Cab/Merlot Reserve
Signature Rosé Reserve
Pinot Noir Reserve
Pinot Noir/Riesling
Cabernet Franc Reserve
Merlot Reserve

White/Sparkling
Artisan Dry Rielsing
Pinot Blanc Reserve
Pinot Grigio Reserve
Riesling Reserve
Riesling/Gris
Dry Riesling Reserve
Gewürztraminer Reserve
Sauvignon Blanc
Naked Chardonnay Reserve
Brys Bubbly

TASTINGS	TAKE HOME	RESERVATIONS
Tower flight: 5 for $17	$18–$55	For more than 8

VISIT

3309 Blue Water Rd. • Traverse City, MI 49686

231.223.9303 • brysestate.com

Open year-round

Cadillac Winery

LEROY · EST. 2013

A taste of country life is on display at the Cadillac Winery. The small red building looks more like a home, and the relaxed atmosphere is continued inside. The long bar is paneled in weathered barnwood, which also roughly frames each window. You can have a seat at the bar, or choose the open air of the pergola out front. The vineyard brushes up against the drive, which is lined with colorful plantings; nature is never far away.

Food trucks are an occasional treat, and special celebrations throughout the year include live music.

POSSIBILITIES

Red/Rosé
Carnal Red
Cellar Red
Frontenac Gris Blush
Marquette
Timberdoodle Royal Red

White
Itasca
Artisan White
Green Apple Riesling
Leahy Riesling

Fruit/Dessert
Crantastic
Pucker Up
Pucker Fizz
Blackberry
Black Currant
Ice Wine
Raspberry Ice
Wildberry

TASTINGS	TAKE HOME	RESERVATIONS
4 for $10	$11–$35	Walk in

VISIT

17480 18 Mile Rd. • LeRoy, Michigan 49655

231.872.9973 • jean@cadillacwinery.com • cadillacwinery.com

Open year-round

Cellar 1914

CENTRAL LAKE · EST. 2015

At the top of a gentle rise, the blue and white tasting room of Cellar 1914 is waiting to welcome visitors interested in spending a lazy afternoon watching the sun slowly descend over Grand Traverse Bay while sipping on their favorite wine or cider. As part of a working farm, there are several buildings in the yard aside from the tasting room, and guests have the opportunity to stay in the farmhouse just across the drive. The roomy bar is paneled with repurposed red board-and-batten, and there are wine barrel tables as well. Outdoors, a large veranda offers the perfect place to stretch out, and a pergola brings shade to the sunny yard. Farm toys are scattered about for their younger visitors, who might also enjoy the bright pink tractor out front. Several games, including cornhole and board games, make this a nice place for families to visit. In winter, bring your outdoor gear and ski or showshoe the trails through the orchards.

Cellar 1914 also has a tasting room in East Jordan (101 Main St.).

POSSIBILITIES

Red/Rosé
Marechal Foch
Reminiscence

White
Snow Daze
La Crescent
Vignoles
Frontenac Blanc

Fruit/Dessert
Cherry
Lake Effect Ice Wine

Hard Cider
Blueberry Apple Cherry
Caramel Apple
Pineapple Habanero
Sea Salt Lime
Peach
Go Green
Honey-crisp
Blackberry
Cranberry Apple

TASTINGS	TAKE HOME	RESERVATIONS
3 for $5	$16–$40	Walk in

VISIT

5833 Shooks Rd. · Central Lake, MI 49622 · 231.676.8743
cheerstothenext100years@cellar1914.com · cellar1914.com
Open year-round

The Cellars of Royal Farms

ELLSWORTH · EST. 1996

R oyal Farms Farm Market hides a lovely secret behind its beautiful red barn exterior. Drive around back and enjoy the tasting room of the Royal Farms Winery. Explore the expansive market, filled with delicious bakery items, lunch offerings such as asparagus soup and cherry chicken salad sandwiches, and all the cherry-themed gifts you could ever desire. But once you've done that, walk up the path on the right side of the building, or simply drive around, and you're ready for round two.

Inside the tasting room, a large bar and scattered tables offer plenty of room for guests. A cozy couch sits in front of the fireplace, and large windows brighten up the space. Outside, a sunny deck offers several seating areas. If you are feeling energetic, climb the hill through the vineyards and catch a beautiful view of Lake Michigan in the distance.

POSSIBILITIES
Red
Rex Beach
White
Sun Kissed
Breezeway
Antrim Creek
Fruit
Brassy Balaton
Cheeky Cherry
Sweet Summer
Hard Cider
Royal Reserve
Pink Bikini
Hand Picked
Hard Red
Botanic
Caramel Apple
Green Apple
Summer Crush

TASTINGS	TAKE HOME	RESERVATIONS
4 for $9	$9–$10	Walk in

VISIT
10445 N. U.S. 131 · Ellsworth, MI 49729
231.599.3222 · royalfarmsinc.com
Open seasonally

Chateau Chantal Winery

TRAVERSE CITY · EST. 1991

Old Mission Peninsula is home to Chateau Chantal, a sprawling French-style winery with a knack for making you feel like you're home. Visitors can soak up the sun on the patio just outside the entryway, where views stretch down the vineyard rows, touching clumps of treetops before soaring over West Grand Traverse Bay. Outside the tasting room, on the opposite side of the building, a similar view tumbles down to the East Bay. Such an embarrassment of riches in one place!

Just inside the entrance is the store, with its beautiful bay windows and seating area, and beyond that the tasting room. The rectangular bar has plenty of room, and there is always the beautiful patio, which doubles the space.

Once you visit you won't want to leave, and that's lucky, because they have a beautiful bed and breakfast available, with all the amenities. Events include Jazz at Sunset on Thursday evenings in the summer months, special wine dinners, and VIP tours.

POSSIBILITIES

Red/Rosé
Pinot Noir
Pinot Noir, Proprietor's Reserve
Trio, Proprietor's Reserve
Cabernet Franc, Proprietor's Reserve
Malbec Reserve

White
Pinot Blanc
Pinot Grigio
Chardonnay
Chardonnay, Proprietor's Reserve
Semi-Dry Riesling

Sparkling
Cherry
Celebrate
Naughty Apple Cider
Naughty Cherry Cider

Fruit and Dessert
Cherry
Cerise Cherry Port

TASTINGS	TAKE HOME	RESERVATIONS
5 for $7	$14–$35	For groups of 6 or more

VISIT

15900 Rue de Vin • Traverse City, MI 49686

231.223.4110 • wine@chateauchantal.com • chateauchantal.com

Open year-round

Chateau Fontaine

LAKE LEELANAU · EST. 1998

Chateau Fontaine's tasting room is a cedar-shingled delight, from its beautiful borders of perennials to the cottage green of the window trim, complete with boxes of flowers spilling over toward the lawn. Relaxing areas abound, and a vine-covered pergola shades visitors from the afternoon sun. A picturesque vista stretches uphill, with a weathered barn and pines in the distance. Depending on the weather and the time of year, tours are possible; however visitors are welcome to stroll through the vineyard whenever they visit.

Another definite perk to this charming place is the complimentary tastings. If your party is larger than eight guests, however, they charge a minimal $3 per person. Groups are limited in size to 18 people.

POSSIBILITIES

Red/Rosé
Pinot Noir
Woodland Red
Big Paw Red
Laughing Waters Dry Rosé

White
Chardonnary
Pinot Gris
Woodland White
Pinot Blanc
Dry Riesling
Gewürztraminer
Semi-Sweet Riesling
Viognier
Grüner Veltliner

Fruit
Cherry
Cherryshine

TASTINGS	TAKE HOME	RESERVATIONS
Complimentary	$12–$30	Walk in

VISIT

2290 S. French Rd. · Lake Leelanau, MI 49653

231.256.0000 · contact through website · chateaufontaine.com

Open year-round

Chateau Grand Traverse

TRAVERSE CITY · EST. 1974

As the oldest winery on Old Mission Peninsula, Chateau Grand Traverse offers a rich tradition of wine making as well as hospitality. Their tasting room is housed in a large ranch-style building complete with red steel roof and covered porch, which provides plenty of tables for groups, and is heated in the cooler months. A sunny patio offers an unobstructed view through the sloping fields to the forest's edge, and beyond the treetops to the blue waters of the bay. The rows of their oldest vineyard are punctuated with deep red rose bushes, adding an additional touch of loveliness to something that is already close to perfect.

Chateau Grand Traverse also offers visitors the opportunity to stay on site at their Inn, which is just down the drive from the winery. Offering several amenities, including private balconies, the inn provides guests with the respite so many of us are looking for.

POSSIBILITIES

Red/Rosé
Gamay Noir
Gamay Noir Limited
Merlot Reserve
Pinot Noir Reserve
Silouette Red

White
Chardonnay
Late Harvest Chardonnay
Block Twelve Riesling
Dry Riesling
Gewürztraminer
Grüner Veltliner
Late Harvest Riesling
Mich Mash Riesling
Mich Mash White
Muscat Ottenel

Fruit
Cherry "Port" Reserve
Cherry Riesling
Cherry

TASTINGS	TAKE HOME	RESERVATIONS
5 for $8	$9–$30	Walk in

VISIT

12239 Center Road • Traverse City, MI 49686

800.283.0247 • info@cgtwines.com • cgtwines.com

Open year-round

Cherry Republic Winery

GLEN ARBOR · EST. 1989

The Cherry Republic location in Glen Arbor is something few visitors want to miss. Beautifully landscaped with thick plantings of shade-loving varieties and bright bursts of color, the property has several buildings that will offer something for everyone. The tasting room is in its own shingle-sided building. There is a large bar, several tables, and a shady deck for enjoying a peaceful break in the midst of a very busy tourist area. Families are welcome, and younger visitors can taste an assortment of cherry soda pop.

The property also includes a Public House, which offers meals as well as desserts, and a large selection of cherry-themed gifts and treats to take home.

POSSIBILITIES

Cherry Wines
Balaton
Sangria
Cherry Spiced Wine
Conservancy
Sunset Blush
Cherry Adore
Aratas
Liberty
Great Hall Noir
Shook

Grape and Cherry Blends
Cherry Red
Abbondanza
Cherry White
Great Hall Riesling
Omaamaayan Cherry Moscato

Hard Cider
Out on a Limb
Loaded Lug

TASTINGS	TAKE HOME	RESERVATIONS
4 for $4	$14–$26	Walk in

VISIT

6026 S. Lake St. • Glen Arbor, MI 49636

231.226.3033 • info@cherryrepublic.com • cherryrepublic.com

Open year-round

Ciccone Vineyard and Winery

SUTTONS BAY · EST. 1995

The charming tasting room of Ciccone Winery is a beautiful green cottage amidst landscaped shrubs, flowering trees, and wavy borders of perennials. The location is a favorite for wedding celebrations, which are held in the picturesque red barn across the drive. Inside, beautiful timber framing draws the eye upwards, while the stone fireplace and comfy leather chairs complete the picture. Outside, a pergola covered with lush flowering vines crowns the patio and sitting area. Farther back, sunny tables on the lawn overlook the red barn and West Grand Traverse Bay in the distance. The patio provides the perfect setting for live music on Thursdays and Sundays, and for the brave among you, there are several open mic nights.

POSSIBILITIES

Red/Rosé
Rosé
Pinot Noir
Lee La Tage
Dolcetto
Cabernet Franc
Classie Red
Grazie

White
Pinot Grigio
Riesling
Chardonnay
Gewürztraminer
Nectar
Pacentro
Sweet Caroline
Starboard

TASTINGS	TAKE HOME	RESERVATIONS
4 for $22	$21–$40	Walk in

VISIT

E. 10343 Hilltop Rd. • Suttons Bay, MI 49682

231.271.5553 • info@cicconevineyard.com • cicconevineyard.com

Open year-round

Crooked Vine Vineyard & Winery

ALANSON · EST. 2013

The curving gravel drive of Crooked Tree Winery is lined with young trees and vineyards beyond. Its red-shingled tasting room has all the charm of a country home; a pergola supports lush vines, while the live-edge siding blends in well with the plantings and containers of annuals dotting the porch. High ceilings and rough-hewn beams add a dramatic touch to the gold interior. The tasting bar has plenty of room for visitors, while outdoors, a wrap-around porch offers a shady spot to enjoy the view. The lawn stretches out to the vineyard at its edge, with picnic tables and a seating area under the shade of a sprawling apple tree. The view is lovely, with a glimpse of the lake surrounded by rolling hills continuing to the horizon.

POSSIBILITIES

Red/Rosé
Marquette Reserve
Barrel Back Red
2 Mom's Blush
Lakeview Red

White
Pet-O-Se-Ga Blanc
Frontenac Gris
Cottage White
L'Arbre Croche

Fruit/Cider
Just Peachy Sangria
Blackberry
Hard Cider

TASTINGS	TAKE HOME	RESERVATIONS
5 for $8	$14–$40	Groups over 6

VISIT

8370 Lakeview Rd. • Alanson, MI 49706

231.203.4790 • crookedvinewinery@gmail.com

crookedvinewinery.com • Open year-round

FarmHouse Vineyards

PETOSKEY · EST. 2020

Down a picturesque gravel road, curving past lakes and through forests and fields, you'll find the charming red barn of the Farm House Vineyards tasting room. Although the bar is small, you can enjoy a flight in the spacious sitting area or on the patio. There is a bocce ball court and seats surrounding a fire pit, with the vineyards just across the drive.

POSSIBILITIES

Red
Marquette
Barnwood Red

White
Black Sheep

The vines look a bit different here than in other vineyards; the gnarled wood is bare of leaves halfway up, creating a beautiful pattern of branches. This is an organic vineyard, and as such uses no pesticides. Because of that, the vineyard can provide grazing for the owners' sheep in the spring and early summer, resulting in a very manicured look. They're removed when the vines begin to droop with fruit, but once harvest is over, they can return to their peaceful vineyard. So choose a glass of your favorite offering and have a seat contemplating the sheep. But don't be surprised if the curious creatures contemplate you right back.

TASTINGS	TAKE HOME	RESERVATIONS
Flight for $10	$25–$31	Walk in

VISIT

8450 Channel Rd. • Petoskey, MI 49770

231.338.6632 • fhvpetoskey@gmail.com • farmhouse-vineyards.com

Open seasonally

French Valley Vineyard

CEDAR · EST. 2000

The drive to French Valley Vineyards takes you past their gray weathered barn, used for special events, to the large white metal tasting room. A beautiful pavillion provides a shady place to enjoy the vineyards nearby, or you can choose a seat on the sunny patio. Inside, visitors are greeted with beautiful post-and-beam architecture, a cozy tiled bar, and a unique ceiling treatment that combines crystal lighting with punched metal for an ever-changing pattern on the beams overhead. Take a seat at one of the saddle stools, or head outside to stretch out.

POSSIBILITIES

Red/Rosé
Pinot Noir
Sweet Razze
Rosé
Pinot Noir Rosé
Merlot
Merlot Reserve
Cabernet Franc & Merlot

White
Pinot Grigio
Stainless Chardonnay
Oaked Chardonnay
Reserve Chardonnay
Semi Dry Riesling
Dry Riesling
Late Harvest Sweet Riesling
Jezebelle

Fruit
Cherry
Jubilee

TASTINGS
Tower flight: 5 for $18

TAKE HOME
$10–$48

RESERVATIONS
8 or more, call first

VISIT
3655 South French Road • Cedar, MI 49621
231.228.2616 • info@fvvineyard.com • fvvineyard.com
Open year-round

Gabriel Farms and Winery

PETOSKEY · EST. 2000

The big green barn of Gabriel Farms is a welcoming destination for lovers of not only wine, but hard cider and beer as well. Visitors are frequently greeted by one of several friendly dogs they have wandering about, and they'll follow you to the tasting room, which is in the basement of the barn. A curving veranda provides a great place to relax, or you can stay inside, where some of the original rock foundations still remain. The spacious bar and tables provide plenty of room for visitors, but there are other areas outdoors as well. The doorway to the upper level is outside, framed by a pair of pergolas resting on a weathered deck. Inside, the beautiful history of the barn remains, with its soaring beams and weathered wood. When it's not reserved for a special event, visitors can have a seat at the tables, or play corn hole on the lawn to the back of the building. Although the barn has been decked out in modern finery, they haven't left their farm roots behind. Visitors can pick their own apples and raspberries when they're in season.

POSSIBILITIES

Red/Rosé
Marquette
Farmhouse Red
Campfire Concord
Dry Rosé
Sweet Rosé

White
Goldie Girl
LaCrescent
Sweet Gabby

Hard Cider
Black Raspberry
Peach
Strawberry Rhubarb

TASTINGS	TAKE HOME	RESERVATIONS
Varied	$25–$36	Groups of 8 or more

VISIT

2800 East Mitchell • Petoskey, MI 49770 • 231.622.8880
gabrielfarms2800@gmail.com • gabrielfarmsandwinery.com
Open year-round

Glen Arbor Wines

GLEN ARBOR · EST. 2017

On a side street in Glen Arbor, a blue and white trimmed home is the tasting room for Glen Arbor wines. Beautiful hardwoods tower over the building, creating a cool, welcoming oasis. Its small front yard offers a seating area, while inside, a large L-shaped bar can fit eight visitors comfortably. Tables round out the indoor seating possibilities. In the back yard, a deck provides a few more seats, and a great location for the musical guests that are often playing here. The lush grass is the perfect place to listen to concerts, or take in a game of bocce ball or badminton. In the winter months, weekly euchre games and pasta pairings are popular offerings.

POSSIBILITIES

Red/Rosé
Sunset Rosé
Liquid Beauty
Farmstead Red

White
Pinot Grigio
Sauvignon Blanc
Chardonnay
Late Harvest Riesling

Bubbly
Blanc de Blanc
Sparkling Riesling

Hard Cider
Peach

TASTINGS	TAKE HOME	RESERVATIONS
5 for $10	$20–$30	Groups over 10

VISIT

5873 S. Lake St. · Glen Arbor, MI 49636

231.835.2196 · glenarborwines@gmail.com · glenarborwines.com

Open year-round

Good Harbor Vineyards

LAKE LEELANAU · EST. 1980

The folks at Good Harbor Vineyards have been growing grapes here for over forty years, and now the family's second generation is stepping up. The cedar-shingled entrance leads to a roomy tasting room that has plenty of areas for groups, with a long bar and separate tables. But the outside space provides the pizzazz. Their grassy front lawn has several seating areas, with an expansive pergola shading half a dozen tables. Relaxing music is piped through the garden, which is bordered by colorful perennials. Large planters overflow with beautiful flowers, and hanging planters finish the look.

POSSIBILITIES

Red/Rosé
Marquette
Collaboration
Harbor Red
Cabernet

White
Dry Riesling
Pinot Gris
Grüner Veltliner
Late Harvest Riesling
Pinot Grigio
Tribute Barrel Fermented Chardonnay
Unoaked Chardonnay
Fishtown White
Trillium

Sparkling
Blanc de Blanc
Blanc de Noirs

Fruit and Cider
Cherry Wine
Cinn-Cider

TASTINGS	TAKE HOME	RESERVATIONS
5 for $6	$10–$45	For more than 10

VISIT

34 S. Manitou Trail · Lake Leelanau, MI 49653

231.256.7165 · tastingroom@goodharbor.com · goodharbor.com

Open year-round

Green Bird Cellars

NORTHPORT · EST. 2014

The fifteen-acre organic farm surrounding the Green Bird Cellars tasting room embodies the spirit of everything they produce. The pale green tasting room is a sunny haven with friendly folks manning the bar; blue metal chairs and tables are arranged in front of a stone fireplace in the center of the room, with fresh bouquets on every table. Outside there is a small patio with hand-crafted chairs and picnic tables beneath bright umbrellas, where you can look out over the vineyards. They also offer tea and soda, a meat and cheese tray, or cookies to round out your visit. Depending on the season, they also offer produce and flowers, along with their farm fresh eggs.

POSSIBILITIES

White/Rosé
Pinot Gris
Traminette Vignoles
Dry Riesling
Unoaked Chardonnay
Gewürztraminer
Cherry
Concord Rosé

Hard Cider
Cider Rye
Chapple Rye
Cin
Angel's Share
Cherry

TASTINGS	TAKE HOME	RESERVATIONS
3 for $15	$15–$28	Walk in

VISIT

9825 E. Engles Rd. · Northport, MI 49670

231.386.5636

Open year-round

Hawkins Farm Cellars

SUTTONS BAY · EST. 2013

Hawkins Farm Cellars is hard to miss, with its arched brown barn, colorful plantings which attract monarchs and bumblebees, and a large yard filled with spinning garden decorations. Walkways lead past shady seating areas to the covered porch, and into what may quickly become a regular stop. They have two distinctive areas for tastings, a bright farm kitchen style with pine floors and plain white shelves, and a contrasting deep red room with lacquer highlights. Hawkins Farm Cellars showcases not only the delicious Michigan wines that they are rightfully proud of, but also authentic Thai cuisine in their restaurant. There is plenty of room for guests at the bars, or stay a while and enjoy a few Asian delicacies, like Beef Satay or Coconut Seafood Soup.

POSSIBILITIES

Red/Rosé
Road Trip
Anticipation
Centennial Red
Free Range Red
Current Attraction
Hawkins Barn Rosé

White
Out to Dry
Leelanau Farm
Fields of Green
By the Pier
Cowin' Around
Yearling

Fruit and Dessert
Blueberry
Cherry
Peach and Honey

Ciders
Green Apple
Cherry Apple
Blueberry

TASTINGS	TAKE HOME	RESERVATIONS
$1 each	$17–$39	Walk in

VISIT

5046 S. West Bay Shore Dr. • Suttons Bay, MI 49682 • 231.271.2221
contact through website • hawkinsfarmcellars.wordpress.com
Open year-round

Hawthorne Vineyards

TRAVERSE CITY · EST. 1996

Hawthorne Vineyards tasting room is perched atop one of the most picturesque places on Old Mission Peninsula. Despite the area's attraction to thousands of people each season, the crowds disappear and you can imagine yourself in a secluded retreat, far away from the hectic bustle of the summer. The views of both the East Bay and West Bay open up as you reach the parking area, surrounded by sweeping fields that gracefully dip down from the woodlands to the side of the building. Its welcoming feel is amplified by the blue and white exterior, curved gables framing expansive windows, and the honey and green tones of the interior. From the patio, views of both bays draw the eye, and a stone fireplace stands ready to head off the northern chill.

They offer a private VIP tour and tasting, which lasts two hours and can accommodate up to eight people ($25 per person, $100 minimum.) Hawthorne is open seasonally, and they suggest visitors check the website for current hours of operation.

POSSIBILITIES

Red/Rosé
Cabernet Franc/Merlot
Reserve Merlot
Gamay
Reserve Pinot Noir
Lemberger

White
Chardonnay
Pinot Grigio
Barrel Reserve Auxerrois
Pinot Blanc
Select Harvet Riesling
Semi-Dry Gewürztraminer
Delish
Tres Belle Chardonnay
Barrel Reserve Chardonnay

Fruit/Sparkling
Cherry Splendor
Splendid Cider
Soirée

TASTINGS	TAKE HOME	RESERVATIONS
5 for $7	$12–$45	Groups of 8 or more

VISIT

1000 Camino Maria Dr. • Traverse City, MI 49686 • 231.929.4206
info@hawthornevineyards.com • hawthornevineyards.com
Open seasonally

Laurentide Winery

LAKE LEELANAU · EST. 2012

On a small hill at the corner of East Duck Lake Road and South French Road sits the tasting room of Laurentide Winery. A sampling of vines grows along a split rail fence, and Japanese Maples arch overhead along the sidewalk. A large pergola provides a shady area to relax with a glass, or head inside where an expansive bar and cozy seating area are waiting to welcome you.

To showcase their award-wining wines (their Riesling recently won double-gold), Laurentide holds monthly small plate menus which pair four courses with wines carefully chosen to enhance the experience. Reservations required.

POSSIBILITIES
Red/Rosé
Reserve Meritage
Bubble de Bubble Cerise
Bubble de Bubble Rosé
White
Riesling
Reserve Chardonnay
Pinot Gris
Sauvignon Blanc
Fumé Blanc
Chardonnay
Emergence White
Sweet Riesling
Bubble de Bubble
Bubble de Bubble Trouble

TASTINGS	TAKE HOME	RESERVATIONS
$5	$15–$45	For groups over 10

VISIT

56 S. French Rd. • Lake Leelanau, MI 49653 • 231.994.2147
info@laurentidewinery.com • laurentidewinery.com
Open year-round

Leelanau Cellars

OMENA · EST. 1974

If you live in Michigan, chances are one of Leelanau Cellars' wines has graced your holiday table a time or two. There's a beautifully designed bottle for any season, and they are a solid choice when trying to please a crowd. But if you're in the area, you must stop at their tasting room on the shores of tiny Omena Bay, on the western side of Grand Traverse Bay.

With a wall of windows facing the turquoise waters, you can feel the beauty of northern Michigan seeping into your bones. Relax inside at the long bar overlooking the lake, and explore their extensive list of offerings, some only available in their tasting room.

For more adventurous visitors, they offer "Bubbly on the Bay", kayak tours of Omena Bay complete with a tasting of their canned wines. You can even catch a bus in Traverse City which will take you directly to the tour. If the wine tastings and kayaking have given you an appetite, right next to the tasting room is Knot Just Another Bar, a full service restaurant with a wide variety of offerings.

POSSIBILITIES

Red/ Rosé
Autumn Harvest
Baco Noir
Cabernet Franc
Great Lakes Red
Meritage
Merlot

White
Chardonnay
Dry Riesling
Gewürztraminer
Late Harvest Riesling
Late Harvest Vidal
Pinot Grigio
Semi-Dry Riesling
Spring Splendor
Sweet White

Sparkling/Dessert
Bubbly Rosé
Great Lakes Red Bubbly
Tall Ship Bubbly Moscato

TASTINGS	TAKE HOME	RESERVATIONS
5 complimentary	$7–$30	Walk in

VISIT

5019 N. West Bay Shore Dr. • Omena, MI 49674

231.386.5201 • info@lwc.wine • lwc.wine

Open year-round

Left Foot Charley

TRAVERSE CITY · EST. 2004

The tasting room of Left Foot Charley is tucked away on the grounds of what was once the Traverse City State Hospital, in a modern, industrial-style building that is reminiscent of an elementary school. The pale brick is broken by huge windows looking out over a shaded patio. The large bar inside offers plenty of room for tastings, and groups can gather at several tables arranged in the back. The wall of windows lets in the dappled sun from the park-like setting surrounding the building.

There are lots of opportunities for private tastings, depending on your group size and the time you have available. They run from $25 to $55 per person, and take place on-site in the barrel room of the winery.

This is a great area to visit if you're looking for a peaceful and relaxing vibe. The Victorian architecture of the nearby original buildings is beautiful, while additional attractions on the expansive grounds include restaurants, coffee shops, a botanical garden, and a farmer's market on select Saturdays.

POSSIBILITIES

Red
Blaufränkisch
Blaufränkisch Reserve

White
Pinot Gris
Dry Riesling
Murmur
Kerner
Island View Vineyard Pinot Blanc
Pinot Blanc
Seventh Hill Farm Riesling

Sparkling
Gitali

Cider
Fortis Maelum
Engle's Ranson
Cinnamon Girl
Henry's Pippin
Antrim County

TASTINGS	TAKE HOME	RESERVATIONS
4 for $15	$8–$40	Walk in, limited to groups of 6 or less

VISIT
806 Red Dr. #100 · Traverse City, MI 49684
231.995.0500 · leftfootcharley.com
Open year-round

Love Wines

LUDINGTON · EST. 2014

A turn-of-the-century building along Ludington's Pere Marquette Lake is the new home of Love Wines. The tasting room houses an expansive knotty pine bar, with tables dotting the large open space. The white tin ceiling brightens the mood, and seasonal table arrangements provide a nice pop of color throughout. There is also outside seating at the modest patio in front, with a view of the lake across the street. Along with their wines, they also serve soda and ice cream floats for visitors of all ages.

POSSIBILITIES

Red
Scarlett
Driftwood
Red After the Beach
Twilight Kiss
Michigan's Chambourcin
Midsummer Night's Dream

White
Stormfront
Michigan's Edelweiss
Michigan's Brianna
Zinful Strawberry
Jasmine Tea with Cantaloupe

Fruit/Dessert
Deep Space Wine
Apple Cider Wine
Toes in the Sand
Dog Days
Queen Anne's Revenge
Beach Bum Blue

TASTINGS	TAKE HOME	RESERVATIONS
6 for $5	$13–$25	Walk in

VISIT
925 S. Washington Ave. • Ludington, MI 49431
231.843.3363
Open year-round

M-22 Glen Arbor

GLEN ARBOR · EST. 2011

Celebrating everything that northern Michigan has to offer, M-22 Glen Arbor also offers a great tasting experience right on main street, where visitors can sample wines they've produced in conjunction with Black Star Farms. Two massive pine trees set off the tall white and black building, which houses a large gift store as well as a tasting bar. They have a roomy outdoor tasting pavilion with a front row view of everything happening in the village of Glen Arbor. A seat around the fire pit is an option, and the area is filled with picnic tables and high tops. In the main building, wine tastings may be an option on a rainy day, and the backyard is ready for laid back entertainment in the form of corn hole or wooden Connect Four. And there to remind you, lest you forget, is the motto of M-22: "It's not just a road, it's a way of life."

POSSIBILITIES

Red/Rosé
Pinot Noir
Vintners Red
M22 Red
Overlook Red
Pinot Noir Rosé

White
Bubbly Brut
Pinot Grigio
Chardonnay
M22 White

Hard Cider
Apple
Cherry Apple

A Traveler's Guide to Michigan Wineries, Cideries, and Meaderies

TASTINGS	TAKE HOME	RESERVATIONS
5 for $10	$18–$34	Walk in

VISIT

6298 W. Western Ave. (M22 Glen Arbor) · Glen Arbor, MI 49636

231.334.4425

Open year-round

Mackinaw Trail Winery

PETOSKEY · EST. 2004

Rolling hills with vineyards stretching to the horizon surround the friendly and welcoming tasting room of Mackinaw Trail Winery. Stacked stone pillars frame the entrance, and the motif is continued inside. The curved black bar takes center stage against the back wall, and the large open area is dotted with plenty of seats. There is a beautiful mosaic table on display, and something even more honored.

An antique wine press prominently placed is the one once used by the patriarch of the family, Philip Stabile. Coming to America from Sicily in the early twentieth century, he couldn't possibly have envisioned what his descendants would make of the family hobby in this new country. Proud wouldn't begin to cover it.

POSSIBILITIES

Red/Rosé
Estate Marquette Rosé
Estate Marquette
Estate Petite Pearl
North Shore Red

White
Unrestricted Late Harvest Riesling
Pinot Gris
East Park Blanc
Sparkling Riesling
Frontenac Gris
Unrestricted Ascension

Fruit/Dessert
Ice Wine
Iced Cider
Cranberry
White Ibis

Hard Cider
Quercus
Batch – 231
Perry

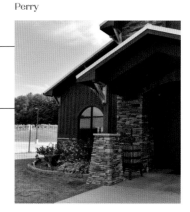

TASTINGS	TAKE HOME	RESERVATIONS
5 for $14	$12–$55	Walk in

VISIT

3423 US Hwy 131 • Petoskey, MI 49770
231.487.1910 • Mackinawtrailwinery.com
Open year-round

Maple Moon Sugarbush and Winery

PETOSKEY · EST. 2015

Billed as "America's First Maple Winery," the friendly folks at Maple Moon surprise visitors with a type of wine they may never have tasted before. But it is well worth a ride in the countryside a few miles east of Petoskey to see what they are up to. The gray, weathered tasting room looks just as you would imagine a sugar shack would, with knotty pine interiors and a granite bar dressing it up inside. Their farm store offers many maple gifts, and visitors of all ages can find something delicious to try, from ice cream in the warmer months to fresh maple candies year-round. Take your treat-of-choice to the deck in back, which overlooks a small patch of wetlands; the maple forest begins at its edge. Tours of the sugarbush are free, but require reservations. In the winter months, try some "wineshoeing". The $25 cost includes a tour, a tasting, and the snowshoes.

POSSIBILITIES

Maple
Early Spring Reserve
Maple Blackberry
Maple Blueberry
Maple Peach
Maple Gold
Maple Royal
Maple Cherry
Red
Maple Rouge
Maple Marquette
Petite Pearl
White
Maple Blanc
Hard Cider
Maple Ginger
Bourbon Aged

TASTINGS	TAKE HOME	RESERVATIONS
4 for $11	$17–$28	Walk in

VISIT

4454 Atkins Rd. • Petoskey, MI 49770

231.487.9058 • mmsyrup.mi@gmail.com • mmsyrup.com

Closed January

Mari Vineyards

TRAVERSE CITY · EST. 2006

Mari Vineyards brings Italy to Old Mission Peninsula in the shape of its beautifully designed tasting room, an Italian villa complete with arched walkways, sunny patios and beautiful stonework. Sweeping lawns provide an expansive view of East Grand Traverse Bay, whether you are outside soaking up the sun, or inside relaxing on a couch. You can't escape this glorious vista.

Charcuterie boards and other small plates are offered, and those interested in a more personal experience can reserve a Mezzanine Tasting for up to 36 people. Walking tours are offered for $25, which includes the production facility and their wine caves, whose intriguing doors you passed as you drove up the hill to the tasting room A private tasting and tour can be reserved for $50. All prices are per person.

POSSIBILITIES
Red
Troglodyte Rosso
White
Pinot Bianco
Bestiary Romata
Stückfass Riesling
Totus Porcus
Late Harvest Riesling
Chardonnay
Scriptorium Riesling
Simplicissimus
Grüner Veltliner

TASTINGS	TAKE HOME	RESERVATIONS
5 for $10	$28–$36	Recommended

VISIT

8175 Center Rd., • Traverse City, MI 49686

231.938.6116 • wine@marivineyards.com • marivineyards.com

Open year-round

Mawby Sparkling Wines

SUTTONS BAY · EST. 1973

If sparkling wines are your thing, then welcome home! Mawby specializes in the bubbly and they've attracted a large following, with good reason. The tasting room is nestled on a small rise, shaded by mature pines and hardwoods, and surrounded by sprawling orchards, vineyards and strips of forest.

You can opt for open air seating inside the building, or on the sunny patio. Either place gives you beautiful vistas of orchards and vineyards gradually climbing the surrounding hills. Large slate steps guide visitors to seating areas near the vineyards, where you can get a closer look at the vines or orchards farther afield.

POSSIBILITIES

Sparkling Red/Rosé
Redd
Grace
Sex

Hard Cider
Bright
Prime
Rooby
Sunlight
Tropic

Sparkling White
Blanc
Detroit
Green
Ca. 2014
Talismon
Us
Gold
Toast

TASTINGS	TAKE HOME	RESERVATIONS
Complimentary	$13–$55	Groups over 8

VISIT

4519 S. Elm Valley Rd. • Suttons Bay, MI 49682

231.271.3522 • info@mawbywine • mawby.wine

Open year-round

Nathaniel Rose Wine

SUTTONS BAY · EST. 2010

The tasting room of Nathaniel Rose Wines is easy to miss; it looks like any other workaday farm on the peninsula, with its overgrown acreage and weathered barn. But if you're interested in wine, and only wine, this is a place for you. They don't stand on ceremony, but the service inside the tiny tasting room is incredibly friendly and knowledgeable. It's a quirky place, and one you probably won't forget. There are a few stand-up tables outside, and the bay is close enough for a walk down to the water's edge.

POSSIBILITIES

Red
Pinot Noir
Right Bank LMS
Right Bank Leelanau
PortChambourcin
De Chaunac
Left Bank
Syrah "La Blonde"

White
Unicorn Sparkling
Marsanne/Rousanne
Dry Traminette
Dry Gewürztraminer
Beerenauslese Riesling

Mead
Pyment

TASTINGS	TAKE HOME	RESERVATIONS
3 for $5	$16–$150	Walk in

VISIT
1865 N. West Bay Shore Dr. • Suttons Bay, MI 49682 • 231.271.5650
info@nathanielrosewine.com • nathanielrosewine.com
Open year-round

Northern Natural Cider House & Winery

KALEVA · EST. 1997

Northern Natural knows how to make cider, and the proof is in the gold medals they have been awarded at the world cider championships, including double gold for their Northern Star. They don't stand on ceremony here, but they've created a charming and friendly tasting room, with a long bar which easily seats ten, and a few tables along the wall. There are two large covered porches, one for food trucks, and one lined with shady seating areas and colorful hanging baskets. The sunny yard beyond is the perfect place to relax and enjoy the occasional concert, munching on an organic pizza or an offering from the food trucks, with an ice-cold cider, of course.

POSSIBILITIES

Red/Rosé
Rockin' Robin Red
Pinot Noir
Pinot Noir Rosé

White
Chardonnay
Riesling
Dry Riesling
Pinot Gris

Fruit/Dessert
Rockin' Robin Cherry
Rockin' Robin Peach
Liquid Gold
Iced Apple Cider
Grape Dessert
Cherry Dessert

Hard Cider
Northern Star
Lavender Apple
Blueberry Apple
Elderberry Apple

TASTINGS	TAKE HOME	RESERVATIONS
$10	Cider: $2.50	Walk in
	Wine: $9–$20	

VISIT

7220 Chief Rd. • Kaleva, MI 49645

231.889.0064 • northernnaturalwinery.com

Open year-round

Peninsula Cellars

TRAVERSE CITY · EST. 1994

Peninsula Cellars tasting room is housed in a charming old school house, circa 1896, complete with its original bell and long narrow windows spanning opposite walls. Those windows, which must have been quite a distraction for students, now create a sunny welcome in the open interior and spacious tasting bar. This is a fun place to visit; the school house theme is carried throughout, from the wines to photo ops for naughty students.

For those who relish the outdoors, there is also a patio where you can relax in the shade of mature maples. This is a beautiful place in the fall especially, when the trees frame the red and white building in all their autumn glory.

POSSIBILITIES

Red/Rosé
Exchange Student
Old School Red
Detention
Homework
Pinot Noir Reserve
Cabernet Franc Merlot Reserve
Lemberger Rosé

White
Dry Riesling
Manigold Gewürztraminer
Chardonnay
Late Harvest Riesling
Old School White
Pinot Grigio
Pinot Blanc

Specialty
Pop Quiz
I'll Drink to That
Hot Rod Cherry

TASTINGS	TAKE HOME	RESERVATIONS
5 for $5	$17–$30	Recommended

VISIT

11480 Center Rd. • Traverse City, MI 49686

231.933.9787 • peninsulacellars.com

Open year-round

Petoskey Farms Vineyard & Winery

PETOSKEY · EST. 2014

The tasting room for Petoskey Farms is in a cute brown farm-style house complete with dormer windows trimmed in red to match the charming cupolas perched atop the building. An expansive covered porch stretches the length of the building, and several decks offer a sunny place to enjoy the scenery. Gentle hills, dotted with vineyards, fields, and clumps of woodland extend out to meet the horizon, completing the picture of a relaxing country retreat.

Thursday evenings in the summer, visitors can enjoy personal wood-fired pizzas with a glass of their favorite wine.

POSSIBILITIES

Red/Rosé
Joy
Petoskey Red
Love Sangria
Marquette MI
Romance
Frontenac Noir
First Crush
Marquette Rosé

White
Pet Nat Front Blanc
Sweet Riesling
Front Gris

Sparkling
Shimmer Red
Shimmer Rosé
Shimmer White

Hard Cider
Honey Apple
Lavender/Ginger

TASTINGS	TAKE HOME	RESERVATIONS
5 for $7	$15–$28	Groups of 8 or more

VISIT

3720 Atkins Rd. · Petoskey, MI 49770

231.290.9463 · staff@petoskeyfarms.com · petoskeyfarms.com

Open year-round

Pleasant Valley Farm and Vineyard

HART · EST. 2015

NORTHWEST

The beautiful red and white barn-style tasting room of the aptly-named Pleasant Valley Farm is situated at the top of a hill, bordered by a beautiful hardwood forest behind it, and a gently sloping vineyard in front. As you approach along the gravel drive, a picturesque lake appears to complete the vision. Inside, the friendly tasting room has a small bar in the front room, with a large open area in the main part of the building. The space is put to good use, with opportunities for group activities such as yoga and paint 'n sip parties. Live music is also an occasional attraction. In the warmer months, the large doors are opened and visitors are part of the natural world around them, the vineyards just a few steps beyond the covered porch, and the sparkling lake just down the hill. Pleasant Valley also offers the opportunity to rent one of several lakeside cottages, each with their own unique appeal.

POSSIBILITIES

Red
Red Trillium
Marquette
Petite Pearl
Sweet Rosé

White
White Trillium
Vidal
Riesling

TASTINGS	TAKE HOME	RESERVATIONS
$6	$16–$25	Walk in, scheduled tasting events only

VISIT

522 N. 69th Ave. • Hart, MI 49420 • 616.288.4229
pleasantvalleyfarmsmi@gmail.com • pleasantvalleyfarmsandvineyard.com
Open seasonally

Pond Hill Farm

HARBOR SPRINGS · EST. 1995

P ond Hill Farms is a delightful stop for travelers visiting the Tunnel of Trees north of Harbor Springs. It has something for everyone, from the winery to the farm-to-table restaurant, to the many activities they offer throughout the changing seasons. Beautiful perennial plantings line the walkways and entrance to the market. Upstairs is the tasting room, which also includes their own beers on tap. Next to the tasting room is a popular restaurant, which prides itself on using the produce from their own land. There is also a patio on the upper level, which offers a relaxing view of the fields and vineyard.

Outside, visitors can take in the vineyards, farm animals, and even a trout pond through a network of groomed trails. Autumn brings the huge pumpkin patch, hay rides, pumpkin bowling, and cider and donuts. Winter offers cross country skiing and snowshoeing on the trails, and a sledding hill for the kids. This is a great destination for families, and everyone will find something they love.

POSSIBILITIES

Red/Rosé
St. Croix
Regatta
Pond Hill
School House
Lakeview Rosé

White
Pinot Gris
Pond Hill White
St. Pepin
Harvest Moon

Specialty
Northern Lights Peach Sparkler
Cherry Wine
Frosted Marquette

Hard Cider
Blueberry
Dry Hopped
Rhubarb
Tunnel Vision

TASTINGS	TAKE HOME	RESERVATIONS
4 for $10	$16–$25	Walk in

VISIT

5699 S. Lake Shore Dr. • Harbor Springs, MI 49740
231.526.3276 • info@pondhill.com • pondhill.com
Open year-round

A Traveler's Guide to Michigan Wineries, Cideries, and Meaderies

Resort Pike Cidery & Winery

PETOSKEY · EST. 2017

The red and white 1889 barn with the huge American flag decorating its side lets you know you've arrived at Resort Pike. If you enjoy sparkling beverages, they specialize in both sparkling ciders and wines. The tasting room, a cozy red square building complete with cupola, is just behind the barn. Inside, the wooden bar dominates the room, and there are a few smaller tables surrounding it, with a variety of board games should the mood strike. The lovely post and beam pergola outside is a great place to relax and watch the tiny goats in their pens nearby. Petting is encouraged.

POSSIBILITIES

Sparkling/Still

Petoskey Brut
East Park Blanc
Sparkling Frontenac Gris
Sparkling Marquette
Sparkling Riesling
Pink Frizzante
Raspberry Fizz
Resort Pike Blanc
Resort Pike Demi-Sec
Resort Pike Rouge

Ciders

Quercus
Batch (231)
Apple Blueberry
Sweet Cameo
Dry Hopped
Cherry Popper
MK's Ultra
Perry

TASTINGS	TAKE HOME	RESERVATIONS
5 for $10	$12–$25	Walk in

VISIT

3471 Resort Pike Rd. • Petoskey, MI 49770

231.753.2508 • contact@resortpike.com • resortpike.com

Open seasonally

Rove Estates

TRAVERSE CITY · EST. 2016

One of the many attractions of northwest Michigan is its beautiful sunsets, and Rove Estate is the perfect place to experience that. It's positioned at the highest point in Leelanau County, and visitors are encouraged to take in the view from their expansive covered porch and viewing platform. The rows of vines gently descend across rolling hills, with bands of green forest disappearing towards the horizon. The tasting room is modern, with a high, angled roof line, but there is also an echo of the past surrounding you. The barnwood used in the décor is from the family homestead, a reminder of a proud past.

Summer includes live music and outdoor games for both kids and adults – yard Jenga and cornhole – and winter offers snowshoeing up the Rove Point trail for more spectacular views, ending with a glass of your favorite wine around a roaring fire.

POSSIBILITIES

Red/Rosé
Cuvée Rosé
Ragaire Rosé
Cabernet Franc Estate
Merlot Estate
Cabernet Franc/Merlot
Tri
Pinot Noir Rosé

White
Gewürztraminer
Sauvignon Blanc
Select Harvest Riesling
Pinot Grigio
Unoaked Chardonnay
Reserve Oaked Chadonnay
Riesling
Brut Sparkling

TASTINGS
5 for $7

TAKE HOME
$17–$35

RESERVATIONS
More than 8 guests

VISIT

7007 E. M-72 • Traverse City, MI 49684

231.421.7001 • info@roveestate.com • roveestate.com

Open year-round

A Traveler's Guide to Michigan Wineries, Cideries, and Meaderies

Rudbeckia Farm and Winery

PETOSKEY · EST. 2015

Housed in a cute gray and white pole barn, the warm and very inviting atmosphere of Rudbeckia Farm caters to visitors of all ages. The open garage door leads to a rustic seating area, paved only with wood chips and leading down to a long patch of lawn. Seating areas are scattered around tables and bonfires, and if you're there at the right time, making S'mores is a definite possibility.

With the laid-back atmosphere of Rudbeckia Farm, it makes the perfect place to relax and stretch your legs. Kids can climb over the play equipment and log benches, or have a game of corn hole. The bocce ball court is a unique attraction that intrigues all visitors. Don't be shy, you might be a natural!

From flatbread pizzas to specialty hotdogs, their menu is small but eclectic. They even offer a S'mores pack to toast your own. Rudbeckia Farm is also home to Toasted Marshmallow Brewstillery, for the spirits and beer lovers in your group.

POSSIBILITIES

Red/Rosé
Belle Rouge
Marquette Dry Rosé
Pinot Noir
Syrah
Sumptuous Sweet Red
Blushing Moscato

White
Bell Blanc
La Crescent
Late Harvest LaCrescent
Cabernet Sauvignon

Specialty
Blanc de Blanc Sparkling
Red Sangria

Cider
Candy Apple
Rellinger Apple
Up in Smoke Pecan Maple Apple
Ginger Root Infused Apple

TASTINGS	TAKE HOME	RESERVATIONS
4 for $16	$21–$50	More than 6 guests

VISIT

3379 Lake Grove Rd. • Petoskey, MI 49770

231.622.4173 • info@rudbeckiafarm.com • rudbeckiawinery.com

Open year-round

Seasons of the North Winery

INDIAN RIVER · EST. 2012

The large tasting room/production facility for Seasons of the North has a unique exterior, part brick, part concrete, which gives it an old-world feel. A large covered porch stretches along the side, with bright red chairs and barrel tables. Cheerful planters and a large landscaped area to the front complete the country look. Inside, it's spacious, with plenty of room at the L-shaped bar and surrounding tables. The winery shares its home with Burt Lake Brewery, so they'll have something for both wine and beer lovers to enjoy. They offer small plates and homemade soup, which makes it a nice stopover on a cold winter's day.

POSSIBILITIES

Red/Rosé
Mullet Lake Mist
The Cabin
Northbound
Backroads
White
River's Edge
Burt Lake Breeze
Lake House
Slopeside
Fruit
Blueberry
Indian Summer Sangria

TASTINGS	TAKE HOME	RESERVATIONS
4 for $5	$16–$20	Walk in

VISIT

9090 M-68 · Indian River, MI 49706

231.548.1280 · seasonsofthenorth@gmail.com · seasonsofthenorth.com

Open year-round

Shady Lane Cellars

SUTTONS BAY · EST. 1996

The charming tasting room for Shady Lane Cellars is a beautiful destination with a quaint history. The repurposed stone building was once a chicken coop, and to prove it, they've even left a small opening which was once used by the birds in question. However, viewing the lovely bi-level building, complete with fireplace and beautiful wood paneling, the last thing you would think of would be a farmer's outbuilding. The interior has a small tasting bar and a gift shop, while outside, a large tasting pavilion offers plenty of room to enjoy the seasons surrounded by hydrangeas and other perennials. Paved patios lead to sunny seating areas or the deep shade of a red maple. An outdoor fireplace provides a bit of warmth on a chilly evening, while towering pines guard the edge of the lawn. Views of the vineyard beyond stretch to the horizon.

Shady Lane Cellars is a popular stop-over for travelers on the Leelanau Bike Trail which joins Suttons Bay and Traverse City. The trail passes by the edge of the estate, making it a perfect break for a drink and perhaps a little live music, if your timing is right.

POSSIBILITIES

Red/Rosé
Pinot Noir
Cabernet Franc
Franc 'n Franc
Blaufrankisch
Pinot Noir Rosé
Coop de Rosé

White
Grüner Veltliner
Pinot Gris
Dry Riesling
Muscat
Semi-Dry Riesling
Pomeranz
Late Harvest Riesling
Coop de Blanc
Sparkling Riesling

TASTINGS	TAKE HOME	RESERVATIONS
3 for $10	$9–$62	Group of 6 or more

VISIT

9580 E. Shady Lane • Suttons Bay, MI 49682

231.947.8865 • info@shadylanecellars.com • shadylanecellars.com

Open year-round

Silver Leaf Vineyard and Winery

SUTTONS BAY · EST. 2015

The tree-lined gravel road leading to Silver Leaf runs between two vineyards and ends at the modest but very friendly tasting room. Its bright yellow walls bring in the sunshine, and its pine bar has plenty of room for several visitors. There are a few seating areas indoors, but there is also a deck with shady umbrellas and a view of the vineyards through the towering pines overhead. There are two miles of trails through the property, and guests are encouraged to explore the landscape. The tranquility of the area is very popular, and there is a cute cabin near the tasting room which can be rented out for those who revel in the sounds of nature with nothing to interfere. During the winter months, snowshoeing and cross-country skiing along the trails are a popular diversion.

POSSIBILITIES

Red/Rosé
Pinot Noir
Cabernet Franc
Fling
White
Chardonnay
Pinot Gris
Riesling
Specialty
Passion
Chafia Cherry
White Sangria

TASTINGS	TAKE HOME	RESERVATIONS
5 for $4	$15–$24	Walk in

VISIT

11087 E. Silver Leaf Farm Rd. • Suttons Bay, MI 49682

231.271.3111 • info@silverleafvineyard.com • silverleafvineyard.com

Open year-round

Soul Squeeze Cellars

LAKE LEELANAU · EST. 2016

From the outside, Soul Squeeze Cellars is a charming blue and white lake house, with gray stone accents and a wall of windows. But inside, they've turned the charm to chic in a beautiful display of modern design. The circular white bar is very roomy, and bottles are displayed inside a separate glassed-in area. Lime-green chairs are set off against walls of white, which give the tasting room an airy, comfortable feeling. A fireplace on the far wall has an inviting seating area where you can enjoy the change in seasons through the windows which frame the white stone. Outside, a sunny patio is dotted with green umbrellas, and the back yard has plenty of room to enjoy lawn games or a nice cozy bonfire during the colder months.

POSSIBILITIES
Red
Parable Petite Sirah
Crazy Carroll Cherry Fortified
White
I Chardonnay
Good Fight Pinot Gris
U Chardonnay
Rapt Riesling
Sparkling
The Pearl Rosé
The Gruve Sparkling Grüner
Hard Cider
Bot Hop
Bip Juniper
Captain Hotpants
Prarie Poet
Boo Cherry

TASTINGS	TAKE HOME	RESERVATIONS
3 for $5	$12–$32	For groups of 10 or more

VISIT
105 E. Philip St. · Lake Leelanau, MI 49653
231.994.2156 · info@soulsqueezecellars.com · soulsqueezecellars.com
Closed January

Spare Key Winery

CHARLEVOIX · EST. 2011

The spacious new tasting room for Spare Key offers several areas for visitors to relax and sample the wines while enjoying the view. A large covered porch looks over the vineyard just a few yards away, while fields and swatches of woodland disappear in the distance. Inside, weathered barnwood has been used to good effect, its angled pattern lining each wall and reaching up to the corrugated metal ceiling. There is plenty of seating at the long bar and surrounding tables, or take a glass to the patio and enjoy the country view.

POSSIBILITIES

Red/Rosé
Frontenac
Marquette
Frontenac/Marquette
Sweet Red

White
Cayuga White
Elvira
Sweet White

Fruit
Apple
Pear
Strawberry
Black Raspberry
Golden Raspberry
Red Raspberry

TASTINGS	TAKE HOME	RESERVATIONS
4 for $7	$15–$30	Walk in

VISIT

06872 Upper Bayshore Rd. • Charlevoix, MI 49720

231.250.7442 • sparekey4@gmail.com • sparekeywinery.com

Open year-round

St. Ambrose Cellars

BEULAH · EST. 2011

The beautiful red barn surrounded by a split rail fence and lush green lawn lets you know you've arrived at one of the most popular meaderies in the state. There's a lot of fun packed into a visit to St. Ambrose. Not only do they have some of the best mead in Michigan, they also offer their own wines and beers, and a wide assortment of burgers, sandwiches and wood fired pizzas, including the "Angry Bee," which is made with a special hot honey sauce. Inside, you can take a seat at the bar for a tasting or grab a booth or table. There is also plenty of room on the enclosed porch or sunny seating around the spacious lawn. There is a beautiful bee garden to explore, as well as a bocce ball court and other yard games. One of their most popular activities is the 9-hole disc golf course, which meanders around the property through a forest of young jack pines. Explore their shop before you go, where you can get your own bottle of that hot honey sauce to take home.

POSSIBILITIES

Red
Quintet
Merlot

White
Dry Riesling
Secret Beach

Still Mead
Star Thistle Ambrosia
Dancing Bare Ambrosia
Cherry Amore

Draft Mead
Razzputin
John Lemon
Black Madonna
Rhythm & Blues

Draft Cyser
Grateful Head
X.R. Cyser
St. Cider

TASTINGS	TAKE HOME	RESERVATIONS
4 for $12	Wine: $15–$37	Walk in
	Mead: $8–$27	

VISIT

841 S. Pioneer Rd. · Beulah, MI 49617

231.383.4262 · stambrose-mead-wine.com

Open year-round

Suttons Bay Ciders

SUTTONS BAY · EST. 2015

Perched on the top of a hill with a beautiful view of West Grand Traverse Bay framed by the hardwood forest, Suttons Bay Ciders is a charming stop on the peninsula. Follow the flagstone walkway past hydrangeas and birch trees to the entrance with its unique canoe crowning the door. Inside, the long bar stretches the length of the room, with a row of windows showing off the view. The patio outside provides a sunny spot to relax, with several levels of stairs descending past an extensive rock garden, complete with rose bushes and apple trees. Beyond the garden, the orchard is inviting, and guests are encouraged to walk through and explore. Adventurous souls in the winter bring their snowshoes for a unique visit to the sleeping orchard.

POSSIBILITIES

Ciders
Sweet Bay
Power Island
Sidra-La Peño
Mosaic
I Spy Ginger
Cherry Fest!
Smitten
Barrel Rider
Highlander
Portal

TASTINGS
4 for $7

TAKE HOME
$8

RESERVATIONS
Walk in

VISIT

10530 E. Hilltop Rd. • Suttons Bay, MI 49682

231.271.6000 • info@suttonsbayciders • suttonsbayciders.com

Open year-round

A Traveler's Guide to Michigan Wineries, Cideries, and Meaderies

Tabone Vineyards

TRAVERSE CITY · EST. 2018

Tabone's distinctive red star decorates the two cupolas of their tasting room, and their bright red roof and white siding makes a beautiful focal point, framed by the vineyards rising behind it. Inside, the soaring ceiling and high windows give it a light and airy feel, and there is plenty of room at the white bar and surrounding tables. Outside, a patio offers a chance to enjoy the sun. Charcuterie plates are an option to accompany your favorite glass, and yard games complete the picture of a relaxing and very welcoming space. Within the last few years, Tabone has won several international awards for their offerings, making it a popular stop for many visitors to the area.

POSSIBILITIES

Red/Rosé
Estate Red
Sweet Red

White
Chardonnay Oaked
"Barrel Strength" Chardonnay
Bubbly Chardonnay
Unoaked Chardonnay
Sweet Harvest Riesling
Pinot Gris
Riesling
Bubbly Riesling
Dry Bubbly Riesling
Sweet Bubbly Riesling

TASTINGS	TAKE HOME	RESERVATIONS
5 for $8	$22–$30	Walk in

VISIT

14916 Peninsula Dr. • Traverse City, MI 49686

231.223.4101 • info@tabonevineyards.com • tabonevineyards.com

Open year-round

Tandem Ciders

SUTTONS BAY · EST. 2010

The gravel drive circles around the tasting room of Tandem Ciders, which is housed in a lovely green barn, complete with an overhanging gable and casement windows open to catch the breeze. Beautiful hollyhocks and hydrangeas complete the charming picture. A long cement ramp stretches up to the front door, and inside, the deep red walls set off the dark wood accents of this friendly and inviting stop. There is room for several visitors at the bar, or take a glass outside and enjoy your choice of seating areas. A lovely courtyard, with nasturtiums spilling over the rocks and young fruit trees providing a thin screen, offers tables with shady umbrellas. There are a few tables in the midst of a copse of trees for more privacy, as well as around a fire pit. Tables near the apple orchard provide a close up look at the twelve different cider varieties that are planted. Corn hole is an option, and darts indoors if the weather turns. Charcuterie plates and other snacks are available, as well.

POSSIBILITIES

Hard Cider
Drifecta
The Greenman
Wanda
Feeling Spicy?
Scrumpy Lil' Woody
Smackintosh
Bee's Dream
The Crabster
Pretty Penny
Farmhouse
Pommeau
Pomona

TASTINGS	TAKE HOME	RESERVATIONS
$1.50 each	$12–$15	Walk in

VISIT

2055 N. Setterbo Rd. • Suttons Bay, MI 49682

231.271.0050 • tandemciders.com

Open year-round

Torch Lake Cellars

BELLAIRE · EST. 2014

The beautiful craftsmanship and location of Torch Lake Cellars make this an attractive destination. The mosaic tiles framing the beautifully arched front doors are repeated on the floor inside, and the windows reveal a view that goes on forever. The highlight of the interior is the gorgeous spiral staircase. Its hand-hewn steps and intricate railing lead visitors up to the viewing area inside the cupola, where you can admire the lake and surrounding vineyards. Other distinctive details include the live oak bar, which has a depiction of Torch Lake on its surface. Outside, a large patio offers a mix of sun and shade, and visitors can take a few practice shots off a golf tee at the edge of the hill beyond the patio, or try their hand at a game of ping pong.

POSSIBILITIES
Red
Zweigelt
French Point Pinot Noir
Shenebuck Baco Noir
White
Deep Water Point Pinot Grigio
Sandbar Chardonnay
Torch Light White
Torch River Late Harvest Riesling
Fruit
Blackberry
Strawberry

TASTINGS	TAKE HOME	RESERVATIONS
6 for $5	$24-$30	Walk in

VISIT

5245 Clam Lake Rd. • Bellaire, MI 49615

231.377.9109 • torchlakecellars@yahoo.com • torchlakecellars.com

Open seasonally

Townline Ciderworks

WILLIAMSBURG · EST. 2015

The rustic charm of Townline Ciderworks isn't just in its weathered wood trim and large reclaimed tables of the tasting room, but in the location of the place itself. The black and white pole barn is nestled between orchards, which line the hills beyond the patio and stretch to the horizon. The patio is a great place to relax in the colorful Adirondack chairs and enjoy the clouds rolling by on a breezy day. Inside, the large windows create a bright and open tasting area, with several large tables surrounding the bar and light snacks available. Live music is a treat on Friday evenings in the warmer months, and when the snow hits, cross-country skiing and snowshoeing are encouraged. Ending the cold day with a glass of cider around a campfire is also smiled upon.

POSSIBILITIES

Hard Cider

Sweet Elise

Smart Alec

Sandra Dee

Big John

Queen Ann

Jay Bird

Giggles

Alma Mater

Wine

Julia and Jennie Cabernet Franc

Julia and Jennie Pinot Grigio

Julia and Jenny Riesling

Julia and Jennie Montmorency Cherry

TASTINGS	TAKE HOME	RESERVATIONS
Complimentary sips	4-pack cider: $15–$20	Walk in
Flights: $12	Wine: $14–$20	

VISIT

11595 U.S. 31 S. • Williamsburg, MI 49690

231.883.5330 • info@townlineciderworks.com • townlineciderworks.com

Open year-round

Two K Farms

SUTTONS BAY · EST. 2018

A stand of towering pines crowns the hill behind the white farmhouse-style Two K tasting room. There is a large sunny patio near the trees, or visitors can have a seat on the covered porch and enjoy the view as the hill sweeps down past the farm and to the beautiful blues of West Grand Traverse Bay. Inside, timber framing along the walls and ceiling contrast with the bright walls, and the large windows facing the bay give it a friendly and welcoming vibe. In the winter months, visitors are encouraged to snowshoe along the trail through the vineyard. Settle around the built-in firepit on the patio and warm up with your favorite award-winning cider.

POSSIBILITIES

Hard Cider
Cherry
New World
Old World
Sangria
Heirloom Ice Cider
Honeycrisp Ice Cider
Russet
Rosé
Kingston Black
Spitzenburg
Dabinett
Ellis Bitter
Apple Pie
Golden Russet

Wine
Riesling
Bubbly Riesling
Leelanau Radler

TASTINGS	TAKE HOME	RESERVATIONS
5 for $7	Wine: $13–$18	Walk in
	6-pack cider: $14–$15	

VISIT

3872 S. West Bay Shore Dr. • Suttons Bay, MI 49682

231.866.4265 • info@twokfarm.com • twokfarms.com

Open year-round

Verterra Winery

LELAND · EST. 2011

A small brick building near the main street in Leland is home to Verterra Winery tasting room. Within walking distance of Fishtown and all of Leland's shopping opportunities, Verterra should definitely be included in a list of places to visit. The patterned brick of the historic building is bisected by a long brick-red awning over the entrance. Inside, a long bar offers visitors a relaxing place to recharge, away from the hustle and bustle of the busy community.

The Ridge at Verterra (8080 N. Swede Road in Northport) also offers wine tastings throughout the warmer months, but be sure to check their hours, as it is a popular wedding venue and closes to the public on those days.

POSSIBILITIES

Red/Rosé
Chaos Red
Pinot Noir
Rosé of Pinot Noir
Reserve Red Cab/Merlot

White
Pinot Gris
Pinot Grigio
Pinot Blanc
Late Harvest Vignoles
Gewürztraminer-Dry
Late Harvest Gewürztraminer
Unoaked Chardonnay
Reserve Chardonnay
Late Harvest Riesling
Dry Riesling

Sparkling
Sparkling Rosé
Chaos Sparkler
Fox Island

TASTINGS
5 for $8

TAKE HOME
Wine: $20–$40
4-pack cider: $24

RESERVATIONS
Walk in

VISIT
103 E. River St. • Leland, MI 49654
231.256.2115 • verterrawinery.com
Open year-round

Vista Ridge Vineyards

ALDEN · EST. 2017

The friendly tasting room of Vista Ridge, "Crushin' It," is in the small town of Alden, on the southeastern shore of Torch Lake. The bright red front door provides a spot of color on the black exterior, and the red is echoed in the plaster walls inside. A stone wall behind the long bar adds some drama, and there is an inviting seating area in front of the window facing the street, where visitors can relax and enjoy the bright space with a nice charcuterie tray. Or have a seat in what can only be described as a throne, an intricately carved wooden chair cushioned in leather. Outside, a shady patio offers wrought iron chairs and tables, complete with red umbrellas.

POSSIBILITIES

Red/Rosé
Cabernet Sauvignon
Tempranillo
Malbec
Merlot
Shiraz

White
Gewürztraminer
Semi-sweet Riesling
White Zinfandel
Moscato
Pinot Grigio

Craft
Kiwi Pear Sauvignon Blanc
Peach Apricot Chardonnay
Black Raspberry Merlot
Cherry Chardonnay
Blueberry White
Vanilla Coffee
Dandelion

TASTINGS
4 for $8

TAKE HOME
$18.50

RESERVATIONS
Walk in

VISIT
9104 Helena Rd. • Alden, MI 49612
231.331.5511 • vistaridgevineyards.com
Open year-round

Walloon Lake Winery

PETOSKEY · EST. 2015

With its weathered timbers and live-edge siding, the tasting room for Walloon Lake Winery has the look of a very successful homestead. The swing on the front porch looks out on a border of hollyhocks and other perennials, with the plantings edged with railroad ties and rustic fenceposts. If you are interested in unique building methods, the cordwood construction of this tasting room is a must-see. Using cedar from their farm as the primary building material, they've created a beautiful pattern both inside and out. The curved bar provides plenty of room for visitors, and there are barrel tables around the room. The vaulted ceiling and row of windows makes it bright and airy, and the large stone fireplace makes it cozy. Outside, the sunny patio has several seating areas and overlooks the vineyard and flowerbeds of this tranquil destination.

POSSIBILITIES

Red/Rosé
Randalls Point Red
Mainsail Red
North Arm Noir
Rosie Rosé
Estate Marquette
Regatta Rosé

White
Windemere White
Smooth Sailing
Between the Buoys Blanc
Village Blanc
Echo Beach
Wildwood

Fruit
End of the Pike Peach
Blackbird Blackberry
Dennis Purple Ribbon Blueberry

TASTINGS
4 for $10

TAKE HOME
$16-$34

RESERVATIONS
For groups larger than 6

VISIT
3149 Intertown Rd. · Petoskey, MI 49770
231.622.8645 · walloonlakewinery.com
Open year-round

WaterFire Vineyards

KEWADIN · EST. 2009

WaterFire Vineyards tasting room sits at the end of a gravel drive in a small pine-sided building, its pergola covering a patio area, with tables and couches inside for chillier weather. But its diminutive size creates a coziness that keeps people coming back. Its offerings aren't extensive either, but they are worth the visit. WaterFire offers several levels of the tasting experience; those that require reservations include private tastings with charcuterie and tour, up to a wine dinner in their cellar room. If you would like to spend even more time here, there is a private vineyard retreat for two which is available for rent.

WaterFire has a unique certification that is very interesting for the future of conservation and agriculture. The Sustainability in Practice program (SIP) requires vineyards to abide by strict protocols before earning the certification. WaterFire was the first vineyard outside California to achieve this level of commitment to conservation.

POSSIBILITIES

Dry Riesling
Off-Dry Riesling
Garnet Red
Cuvee Blanc
Dry Apple Cider

TASTINGS	TAKE HOME	RESERVATIONS
$6.50	$25–$32	Walk in

VISIT

12180 Sutter Rd. · Kewadin, MI 49648

231.360.7394 · info@waterfirewine.com · waterfirewine.com

Closed January

Willow Vineyards

SUTTONS BAY · EST. 1998

The fairy tale cottage of Willow Vineyards tasting room is a charming destination in a stunning landscape. Looking out across the vineyards and trees, the view stretches to the waters of West Grand Traverse Bay. Cedar shingles cover the roof and gables and blend with the soft greens of the siding and flower beds. The informal plantings welcome visitors as lavender bushes spill over the gravel drive. You can enjoy a flight at the L-shaped bar inside, or stretch out on the sunny patio. The Wine Shop offers a few snacks, as well as unique items sure to catch your eye.

POSSIBILITIES

Red/Rosé
Pinot Noir
Pinot Noir Rosé

White
Chardonnay
Pinot Gris
Sweet Rain Chardonnay
Road Trip Riesling

Fruit
Balaton Baby Cherry

TASTINGS	TAKE HOME	RESERVATIONS
$1 each	$19–$23	Walk in

VISIT

10702 E. Hilltop Rd. · Suttons Bay, MI 49682

231.271.4810 · willowvineyard@outlook.com · willowvineyardwine.com

Open seasonally

Distilleries of Northwest Michigan

Iron Fish Distillery
14234 Dzuibanek Rd., Thompsonville, MI 49683
231.378.3474
Gin, Vodka, Bourbon, Rum, Liqueur

Grand Traverse Distillery
Tasting rooms in downtown Traverse City, Leland, Mackinaw City
781 Industrial Cir, Suite 5, Traverse City, MI 49686
231.947.8635
Vodka, Whiskey, Bourbon, Gin, Rum

Black Star Farms Distillery
10844 E Revold Rd., Suttons Bay, MI 49682
231.944.1270
Brandy

High Five Spirits Distillery
312 Howard Street, Petoskey, Michigan 49770
231.881.9881
Vodka, Gin, Rum, Whiskey

Traverse City Whiskey Co.
Tasting room in the Stillhouse Cocktail Bar
201 E 14th St, Traverse City, MI 49684
231.922.8292
Whiskey

Northern Latitudes Distillery
112 E. Philip St. (M-204), Lake Leelanau, MI 49653
231.256.2700
Whiskey, Brandy, Gin, Vodka, Rum, Moonshine, Liqueur

Mammoth Distilling
Tasting Rooms in Bellaire, Bay Harbor, Adrian, and Central Lake
221 W. Garland Suite D, Traverse City, MI 49684
231.943.1073
Vodka, Whiskey, Bourbon, Gin, Rum

Ethanology Distillery
127 Ames St, Elk Rapids, MI 49629
231.498.2800
Vodka, Gin, Whiskey

UPPER
PENINSULA

Upper Peninsula

Distilleries of the Upper Peninsula

Les Cheneaux Distillers
172 S. Meridian St./P.O. Box 126, Cedarville, MI 49719
906.484.1213
Vodka, Gin, Whiskey

1668 Winery

SAULT STE. MARIE · EST. 2015

The tasting room for 1668 Winery shares space with the Soo Brewing Company, and with their menu of pizza, burgers, sandwiches and appetizers, there is something here for even the most finicky. The large L-shaped bar dominates the room, and there are several tables filling the space. In the warmer months, visitors can take a glass to the back deck and watch the freighters moving through the locks along the St. Mary's River, and in winter, the hardiest can have a seat around the bonfire out front. The arts play a part at 1668, and live music is a frequent treat. First Fridays are a nod to the artists of the Soo, where visitors can meet the artists and admire the artwork for sale adorning the walls. You may even leave with your own masterpiece.

POSSIBILITIES

Red/Rosé
Pinot Noir
Malbec
White Zinfandel
Pink Moscato

White
Gewürztraminer
Pinot Grigio
Riesling

Fruit
Black Raspberry
Black Cherry
Green Apple
White Cranberry

TASTINGS	TAKE HOME	RESERVATIONS
$1.50 each	$12-$16	Walk in

VISIT

100 W. Portage Ave. · Sault Ste. Marie, MI 49783

906.259.5035 · 1668winery.com

Open year-round

End of the Road Winery

GERMFASK · EST. 2016

They were serious when they named this the End of the Road Winery. Five miles southeast of Germfask and ten miles northeast of Blaney Park, their tasting room sits at the end of a beautiful, if unremarkable, country road. You won't accidently come across this place, you need to really want to find it. But you will want to.

The building is cozy, with a gambrel roof and a patio out front. Their All That Crazz, a blend of cranberry and raspberry, won a gold medal at the 2019 Michigan Wine Competition. That same year, the family planted 490 apple trees and hope to have a hard cider offering in the not-too-distant future.

This is a popular destination for visitors to the area; if you take the time to stop by, you will have truly found a hidden gem.

POSSIBILITIES

Red
Frontenac
Marquette
Big Rosso

White
Intrigued
Benvenuto
Frontenac Gris

Fruit
Blue Phoenix
Blackberry
Sunburst
All That Crazz
Son of a Peach
Mount Me Cherry
Northern Lights Blush
All Bark and No Bite
Tahqua Rush

TASTINGS
5 for $5

TAKE HOME
$13–$15

RESERVATIONS
Walk in

VISIT

6917 Burns Rd. · Germfask, MI 49836

906.450.1541 · 48rbarker@gmail.com

endoftheroadwinerymi.com

Open seasonally

Leigh's Garden Winery

ESCANABA · EST. 2008

The pastel green storefront in downtown Escanaba does not hint at what lies within. Enter and you'll discover the beautiful and spacious tasting room of Leigh's Garden Winery.

The long oak bar stretches most of the way down the first room, and there are inviting arrangements of black leather chairs for more private conversations. The second room, divided from the first by colorful stained-glass panels and a wooden archway, offers tables which can be rearranged for larger groups.

The design of the tin ceiling is echoed on the walls and around the bar. There is an eclectic mix of styles found throughout, from the murals in the back room to the painted floor and curved lights in the front, but they all combine to create a delightful and very welcoming ambiance.

POSSIBILITIES

Red
Marquette
Marquette Noir
Frontenac
Mary Terry
Escanaba Electric Street
Cordwood Johnson
Burly Jack Usimaki
Yooper Reflections

White
Pearl: Our Muse
Gathering
Snow Day
Frontenac Gris
Late Harvest Frontenac Gris
Rocco's Brianna

Seasonal
Red Hot Rhubarb
Pretty in Peach
Strawberry Moon
Hiawatha Blue
Midnight Cherry

TASTINGS	TAKE HOME	RESERVATIONS
6 for $7	$15–$30	Walk in

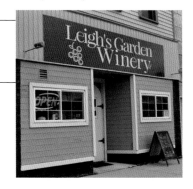

VISIT

904 Ludington St. • Escanaba, MI 49829

906.553.7799 • julie@leighsgarden.com • leighsgarden.com

Open year-round

Northern Sun Winery

BARK RIVER · EST. 2012

The French Provincial–style tasting room welcomes visitors with a path winding through plantings of perennials and leads to the rear of the building, where the vista opens onto their vineyards. Official greeter Smitty, their mature golden lab, might wander over to check things out, but will remain discreetly in the background.

Through the heavy oak door visitors will find a quaint, pine-paneled tasting room with a soaring ceiling, while high windows bring in that Northern Sun vibe. Enjoy a glass outdoors on their vine-covered pergola overlooking the vineyard and nearby barn.

They have been growing vines since 1999, and established the winery in 2012. "Northern Sun Winery," says proprietor Susie Anthony, "is entirely estate grown, produced, and bottled. Something to be proud of wherever the winery is, but we feel it's especially significant here in the U.P.!"

Visitors are welcome to take a self-guided tour of the vineyard. They also offer an outdoor concert series in the summer months.

POSSIBILITIES

Red
Leon Millet
Marquette
Sole Di Sera

Rosé
Rosé

White
Sur-Lie Frog
Ragazza Di Sole
La Crescent
Brianna

Fruit
Rhubarb
Pater Familias

TASTINGS	TAKE HOME	RESERVATIONS
3 for $5	$15–$21	Groups of 10 or more

VISIT

983 10th Rd. · Bark River, MI 49807

906.399.9212 · northernsunwinery@mail.com · northernsunwinery.com

Open year-round

Superior Coast Winery

SAULT STE. MARIE · EST. 2005

The tasting room of Lake Superior Winery is housed in Karl's Kitchen, one of the best-placed restaurants in the Soo. It is shaped like one of the area's ubiquitous freighters, with a prow front and a pilot house sprouting above the roofline. There is a rooftop area which would make the perfect place to relax on a sunny summer day and watch the freighters pass by within a stone's throw. The interior is paneled through wall and ceiling, while the corners of each of the large windows surrounding the building are curved to resemble the freighters, which diners can see passing in front of the building.

The small bar seats four, but there is plenty of room to have a tasting at the tables. Time your visit right, and you can enjoy a meal with a bit of gourmet flair. Chef Karl makes good use of the wines and ales he has and offers a Beer Cheese, Stout Braised Rueben, and Shiraz Stroganoff, just a few items from an eclectic and delicious menu.

POSSIBILITIES

Red/Rosé
Not Your White Zinfandel
Chilean Malbec
Superior Sunset
Lake Superior Red
Agawa Bay Red
Da Yooper Red
Shipwreck Blush

White
Southern Superior White
River Rapids
Autumn Gold
Superior Sunrise

Fruit
Blueberry
White Cranberry
Green Apple
Lily's Poppin' Pomegranate

TASTINGS	TAKE HOME	RESERVATIONS
4 for $11	$13–$21	Walk in

VISIT

inside Karl's Cuisine • 447 Portage Ave. • Sault Ste. Marie, MI 49783
906.253.1900 • info@karlscuisine.com • karlscuisine.com
Open year-round

Threefold Vine Winery

STEPHENSON · EST. 2006

Threefold Vine has taken over the former bank in downtown Stephenson, and it's a perfect venue for showcasing their creations. Imposing columns frame the door, and the classic proscenium arch tops the façade. Inside, the space soars and tall windows flanking the south fill the room with natural light. A small gift area is tucked away to the side. The open design leaves plenty of room for sitting in an armchair enjoying a glass with a friend, or just having a taste at the bar, which deserves a second look. Colorful panels of stained glass are displayed beneath the clear top of the bar, creating a mix of modern and historical design.

Threefold Vine was the first Upper Peninsula winery to make their product from their own U.P.-grown grapes, fruit, and honey.

POSSIBILITIES

Rose
Yooper Cheer

White
Northern Summer
Da White
Brianna
Lorelei

Fruit
Crabby Apple
Happy Apple
Cranberry Crush

Mead
Blackberry
Regular
Purple Bee Pyment
Black Bear Jamboree
Fence Row
Autumn Joy
Summer Island
Copper Country Blues
Glory Bee

TASTINGS	TAKE HOME	RESERVATIONS
Complimentary	$9–$18	Groups of 10 or more

VISIT

S232 Menominee St. • Stephenson, MI 49887 • 906.753.6000
threefoldvine@hotmail.com • exploringthenorth.com/threefold/vine.html
Open year-round

Yooper Winery

MENOMINEE · EST. 2016

If you enjoy a good fruit wine, this winery should definitely be on your radar. At the Yooper Winery, fruit is their specialty; in 2019 their Little Portal Point plum wine won Best of Class in the Michigan Wine and Spirits Competition.

Shaded by hardwoods and a few towering pines, the tasting room entrance is on the side of the dark brown building, with a ramp for easy access. You'll pass through a hallway to get to the tasting bar, where windows offer a glimpse of the production facilities behind the scenes; displays highlight awards and bottles are labeled with descriptions of each wine they offer. A small gift area leads to the bar, where tastes are complimentary and a glass of your favorite is $5. Bottles run from $13 to $20.

POSSIBILITIES

Red
Smashing Red
Merlot
Cheesehead Red

White
Pinot Grigio
Chardonnay
Riesling

Fruit/Dessert
Lights Out
Yooper Stooper
Yooper Blue
Strawberry
Strawberry Rhubarb
Little Portal Point
Raspberry
Cherry Cherry Baby
Red Currant
Old Mack Honey Peach
Cranberry

TASTINGS	TAKE HOME	RESERVATIONS
Complimentary	$13–$20	Walk in

VISIT

915 48th Ave. • Menominee, MI 49858

906.361.0318 • jrl660@hotmail.com • yooperwinery.com

Open seasonally

NORTHEAST

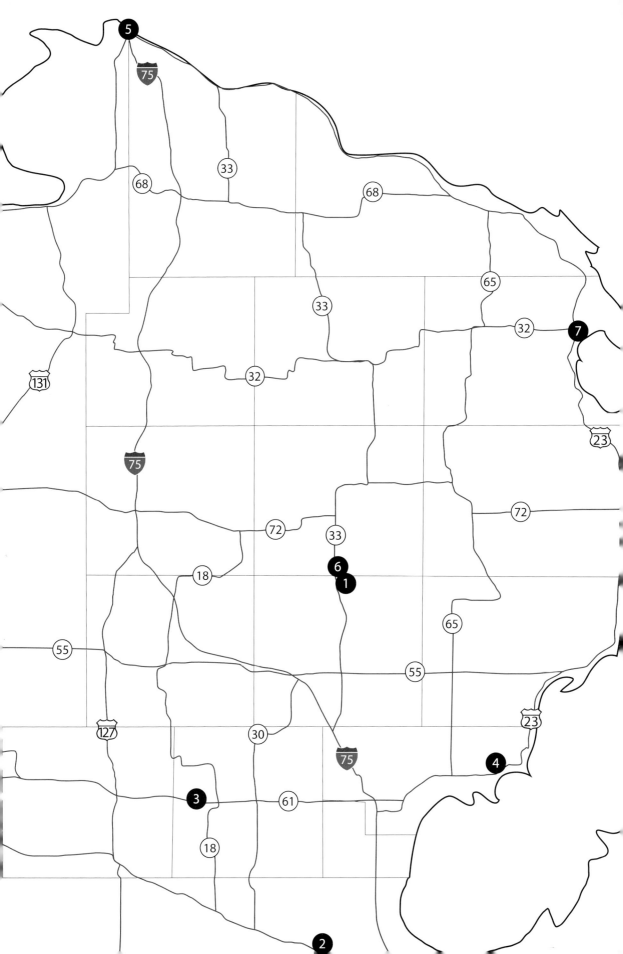

Northeast Michigan

Distilleries of the Northeast

Copper Kettle Distilling

939 West Houghton Lake Drive, Prudenville, MI 48651

989.302.8200

Whiskey, Rum, Vodka, Gin, Liqueur

Country Corner Winery

ROSE CITY · EST. 2022

Housed in a building that has been in the family for generations, the sage green tasting room of Country Corner Winery is a mix of modern and historical, with the soft browns of the century-old wooden floor brushing up against the gray steel and heavy granite bar. Beams overhead complete the look. There is plenty of room at the bar, as well as a few tables scattered around the room. Outside, there are plans to complete the raised veranda, which will provide a sunny option for visitors.

Originally called Valley Mist Winery, its recent purchase resulted in a move for the tasting room to its more convenient location at the corner of M-33 and Houghton Creek Rd., which really is a beautiful country corner.

POSSIBILITIES

Red/Rosé
Red Dress
Cab Stand
Laid Back
Mossberry Dreams
Gabriel
The Swill of a Lonely Red Neck Sailor
Embers
Pink Carnation

White
Moon Danza
Oyster Rd.
Manderina
Green Apples
Razz
Lightening Bug Lemon Wine

Fruit/Dessert
Time Slows (Elderberry)
Snowflake

TASTINGS	TAKE HOME	RESERVATIONS
5 for $5	$14–$35	Walk in

VISIT

2498 N. M-33 • Rose City, MI 48654

989.965.6395 • countrycornerwinery@gmail.com

facebook.com/valleymisttastingroom

Open year-round

Grape Beginnings Winery

MIDLAND · EST. 2015

Downtown Midland has a variety of shops and eateries, and one that you shouldn't miss is the Grape Beginnings tasting room. They specialize in importing juices from around the world, and adding their special Michigan touch as they create their wines on-site. There is an outdoor patio to enjoy a little people-watching, or take a seat indoors at the small bar or a cozy table. After your tasting, choose a favorite to accompany a meal; food offerings include both hot and cold appetizers, soup, flatbread pizza and Nannie's meatballs. The tasting room is just a block away from the Tridge and its riverside park, which makes a great after-dinner destination.

POSSIBILITIES

Red/Rosé
After Hours
Cozy Nights
Dangerous
Down Time
Fury
Jo
Joann
Majestik
Mellow on Main Street
Midland Tri-Umph
Mon Cheri
Notes of Romance
Sweet Intrigue
Temptress
Top Hat
Zenful

White
Bad to the Bone
Blondie
Down Under
Night Cap
Party Time
Petoskey Proud
River's Edge White
Serenity
Sinfully Sweet
The G (Spot)
White Shadow
In addition to Fruit Wines, Dessert Wines, and Meads

TASTINGS	TAKE HOME	RESERVATIONS
2 complimentary, then $1 ea.	$12–$17	Walk in

VISIT

244 E. Main St. • Midland, MI 48640 • 989.486.9569

gbw@grapebeginningswinery.com • grapebeginningswinery.com

Open year-round

The Merry-Hearted Cidery

GLADWIN · EST. 2016

The cozy red tasting room of The Merry-Hearted Cidery is a very friendly country place, complete with covered patio and a frame of split rail fencing. Rosebushes bend over the weathered fenceposts, and large hydrangea provides the perfect backdrop. Inside, the live-edge bar provides standing room for several visitors, or there are seats on the patio out front. The apples for the cider are grown on site, as part of The Fruitful Orchard and Cider Mill. Just across the drive, their gift shop and bakery open in the fall, offering freshly baked pies, donuts, and breads. They also offer the opportunity to pick your own apples, as well as hayrides through the expansive orchard every Saturday, weather permitting.

POSSIBILITIES

Hard Cider
Heartless
Heartfelt
Sweetheart
Chapple
Hoppy Hearted
Black Heart
Heart Throb
Purple Heart
Pear of Hearts
"Grape"ful Heart
Heart of Cin
Strawberry Feels Forever
Chopped
Cinnamon-Pear
Whole Hearted Pearberry
Peach of My Heart
Out of the Blue
Distill My Heart
Pearberry
Coco-Hearted

TASTINGS	TAKE HOME	RESERVATIONS
4 for $6.50	$14–$15	Walk in

VISIT

5740 W. M-61 · Gladwin, MI 48624 · 989.578.2225

drink@localhardcider.com · localhardcider.com

Open year-round

Modern Craft Wine

AU GRES · EST. 2013

The idea that we can participate in creating our own favorite drink is an intriguing one, and it is the foundation of Modern Craft Winery. Visitors have the option of tasting an original wine, combining wines, or adding the wine to another beverage altogether. Recipes abound, but there are flavor combinations yet to be discovered. The original tasting room, in Au Gres, is an unassuming orange and white storefront that hides a stylish but cozy place to relax among friends. The long live edge bar runs the length of the room, and there is a black leather sitting area where creative types can let loose on the chalk walls surrounding them.

Modern Craft Wine also has tasting rooms in Portland (145 Kent St., 517.515.5517), West Branch (224 W. Houghton Ave., 989.345.5226), Milan (42 E. Main St., 734.628.7185), Frankenmuth (925 S. Main St., 989.652.3566), and Wyandotte (109 Maple St., 734.486.6538).

POSSIBILITIES

Red
All Night Red
Au Sable River Red
Fudge

White
Northbound White
Northbound Fall
White Lemon

Fruit/Specialty
Apple
Black Ice
Blackberry
Cherry
Grapefruit
Grapesicle
Mandarin
Peach
Raspberry
Tropical Fruit
Piña Colada
White Glacier

TASTINGS	TAKE HOME	RESERVATIONS
5 for $6	$12–$20	Walk in

VISIT

211 E. Huron Rd. • Au Gres, MI 48703 • 989.876.4948
moderncraftwine.com
Open year-round

Nicholas's Black River Vineyard & Winery

CHEBOYGAN · EST. 1999

For wines produced in the Greek style, with added spices and herbs, look no further than the tip of the mitt. Cheboygan is home to Nicholas's Black River vineyard and production facility, and visitors can taste the wares as well as tour the facility. Murals surrounding the vats of wine illustrate the story of the original winemaker, Nicholas, and his arrival in America in 1951. A small table is reserved for tastings, but if you want a roomier tasting experience, you'll have to visit their Mackinaw City location at the open-air mall of Mackinaw Crossings. An antique bar provides a focal point to showcase their offerings, and a beautiful gift selection decorates the shelves. In the summer months, music wafts in from the bandstand across the lawn.

POSSIBILITIES

Red/Rosé

Valiant
Black River Red
Nicolette Le Blush
Nick's Dry Red
Ten Point
Ambrosia
Mighty Mac
Merlot
Cabernet Sauvignon

White/Fruit

White Zinfandel
Old Mackinac Point Lighthouse
Riesling
Chardonnay
Dionysos
Somewhere in Wine
White Ice Wine
Sweet Temptation
Pear & Share

TASTINGS	TAKE HOME	RESERVATIONS
3 complimentary	$15–$23	Walk in

VISIT

6209 N. Black River Rd. · Cheboygan, MI 49721 · 231.625.9060
nicholas.winery@att.net · nicholasblackriverwinery.com
Open year-round

Rose Valley Winery

ROSE CITY · EST. 2007

Located on a back street in the small town of Rose City, an arbor of grape vines greets visitors to Rose Valley Winery, and an inviting array of perennials and hanging baskets complete the country look. Inside, the bar stretches along the length of the room, with a second room at the back to accommodate larger groups, who are always welcome. This pine-paneled back room, referred to as the "Knotty Room", offers a cozy nook with a gas fireplace and a large table. Windows overlook the production floor, and the owner is happy to give tours of the facility if time allows.

They also have a tasting room in West Branch (West Branch Outlet Shops, 989.726.5018).

POSSIBILITIES

Red
Baco Noir
Devil's Spicy Red
St. Croix
Winter Trails
Rifle River Red
Marquette
Bear Creek

White
Lake Ogemaw
Prairie Star
Sauvignon Blanc
Chardonel
Grayling Gold
Frost Lake

Dessert
Left Side of the Boat
Loon Lake
Nectar of the Woods

Fruit
Bad Apple
Blackberry
Rhubarb

TASTINGS	TAKE HOME	RESERVATIONS
6 for $5	$10–$44	Walk in

VISIT

3039 Beechwood Rd. • Rose City, MI 48654 • 989.685.9399
rosevalley2007@yahoo.com • rosevalleywinery.net
Open year-round

Thunder Bay Winery

ALPENA · EST. 2012

I you've ever wondered what a wine created from Saskatoon berries would taste like, then this is the place for you. The bright yellow tasting room of Thunder Bay Winery is a welcome stop for shoppers in downtown Alpena. The L-shaped bar extends the length of the room, with plenty of seating areas surrounding it. Tall store-front windows provide a view of the outside patio area and the street beyond. Architectural details have been left intact, and the tin ceiling, thin pillars and original wooden floor give it an historical feel. Live music is an occasional treat.

They also offer a tasting room in Petoskey (438 Mitchell St., 231.622.8563).

POSSIBILITIES

Red/Rosé
Marechal Foch
Chambourcin
Rockport Red
Cabernet Franc
Cabernet Sauvignon/Zinfandel

White
Chardonel
Clatter
Chardonnay
Traminette
Pinot Grigio

Dessert/Sparkling
Lighthouse White
Sparkling Raspberry
Harbor of Alpena

Fruit
Cherry
Black Currant
Cranberry

TASTINGS	TAKE HOME	RESERVATIONS
6 for $6	$12–$42	Walk in

VISIT

109 N. Second St. • Alpena, MI 49707 • 989.358.9463
wine@thunderbaywinery.com • thunderbaywinery.com
Open year-round

SOUTHEAST

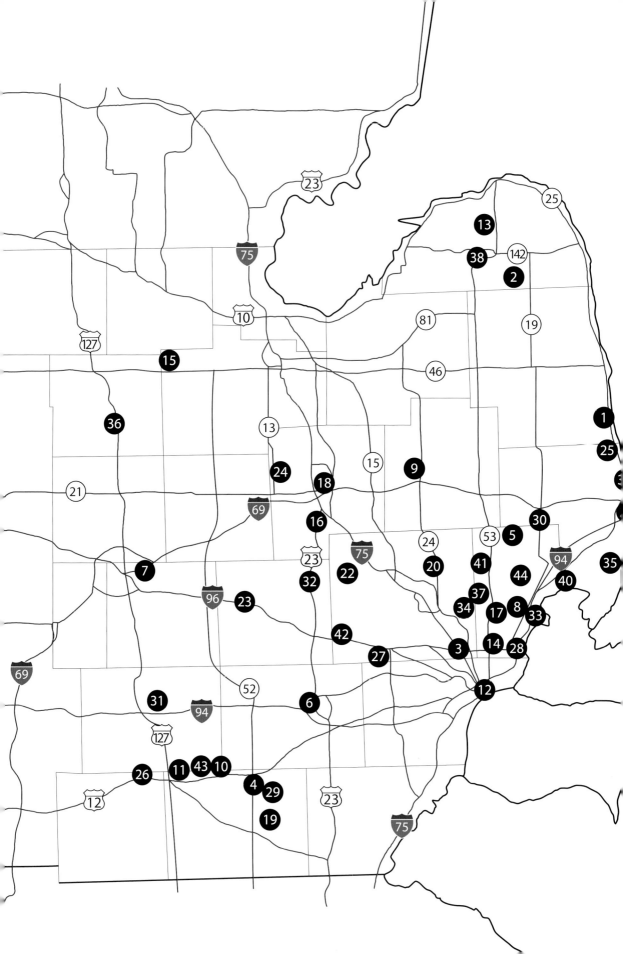

Southeast Michigan

3 North Vines

CROSWELL · EST. 2014

Between the small towns of Croswell and Lexington in Michigan's thumb, past groves of hardwoods and fields of wheat, 3 North Vines tasting room is waiting to show you what country relaxation is all about. Perched on a small rise at the end of a gravel drive, the grey weathered building offers plenty of room to sample their wares, either inside at the bar, or outside at the patio. Groups of green wooden rocking chairs wait within arm's reach of the shady apple trees surrounding it, while the vineyard brushes up against the lawn just a few feet away.

There is an inviting bike path which runs from Croswell in the west to Lexington, on the shore of Lake Huron. When spring fever hits, the 10-mile round trip is a beautiful opportunity to enjoy some fresh country air, and 3 North Vines is the perfect midway point to pause for a light snack and a flight of your favorites. They offer a few meat and cheese trays, along with an assortment of sweets and breads for dipping.

POSSIBILITIES

Red/Rosé
Fool Me Once
X Marks the Spot
Pinot Noir
Pinot Noir Black
Marquette
Marquette Black

White
Lucky Shoe
Seyval Blanc
Riesling

Hard Cider
A Few Good Apples
Espresso Royale
Clear and Present Cider
Lemons Like Us
Cherry Is Not Enough

TASTINGS	TAKE HOME	RESERVATIONS
4 for $7.50	$19–$28	Walk in

VISIT

5940 Peck Rd. • Croswell, MI 48422

810.956.2706 • 3northvines.com

Open year-round

B & B Wines

BAD AXE · EST. 2018

For the perfect country ambiance, head on over to B & B Wines. An inviting path curves behind the house, leading you to a spacious covered patio within sight of the sheep that are grazing in their own separate area. The tasting room has a small bar, but several seating areas throughout. Weathered siding along the wall blends with the steel roof and exposed beams above. A string of happy lights makes this a mellow country experience.

And more experiences await for those who are interested in country crafts. Workshops in basket weaving, wool spinning and glass painting throughout the year attract visitors who want to explore these creative endeavors. Everything is geared towards a natural product, most especially the wines. The owners are happy to share their love for experimenting with flavors and excited about ideas that are just in the planning stage. This is a sweet place to stop, in more ways than one.

POSSIBILITIES

Fruit
Blackout
Midnight Run
Relaxer
The Fuzz
Naked
Naturally Sexy
The Pitts
P.P.
Pineapple Xpress
Stumble

TASTINGS	TAKE HOME	RESERVATIONS
5 for $5	$15–$19	Groups over 10

VISIT

4320 S. Bad Axe Rd. • Bad Axe, MI 48413 • 989.658.8387
michiganpleasures@gmail.com • facebook.com/pg/barbandbob
Open year-round

B. Nektar Meadery

FERNDALE · EST. 2008

The perks of repurposing an industrial space includes having the space to spread out; the tasting room of B. Nektar includes two large seating areas as well as the expansive bar that dominates one end of the room. A narrow outdoor space street-side is available, complete with cornhole and picnic tables. Weekends often include food trucks, while regular themed trivia nights give visitors the chance to donate to a good cause while testing their expertise in various cultural touchstones, such as *The Princess Bride* and *Mean Girls*.

This very inclusive space invites everyone to explore the creative twists they take with their meads, ciders, and wines. They've been included in the ranks of the top 100 breweries world-wide, but they haven't let success mess with their ability to experiment and deliver unique flavors and a fun-loving attitude.

POSSIBILITIES

Mead
Apple Pi
Black Fang
Sunrise Bay
Blackberry Mint
Fleur De Bees
Kill All the Golfers
Optimism
Episode 13
Cherry Chipotle
Pineapple Coconut Express
Cherry Limeade
Dragons Are Real

Cider
The Dude's Rug
Blood Amulet
Core Crusher
Zombie Killer
Death Unicorn
Stupid Man Suit
Slice of Life

TASTINGS	TAKE HOME	RESERVATIONS
$2–$4 each	4-pack: $15	Over 6

VISIT

1511 Jarvis St. • Ferndale, MI 48220

313.744.6323 • info@bnektar.com • bnektar.com

Open year-round

Black Fire Winery

TECUMSEH · EST. 2016

Sitting on a gentle rise beneath the dappled shade of maples and other hardwoods, Black Fire Winery tasting room is an inviting destination for visitors. Its dark brown siding and sage green accents blend into its natural surroundings, and a ramp to the front door makes it accessible to all. There is a pull up for visitors to be let out close to this ramp, but all parking is below the hill a short distance away. The cozy yellow interior includes an L-shaped bar and several tables, while a covered deck off the back looks out over the sunny vineyards beyond.

Weekends often include live music with an eclectic mix throughout the season. Concerts on the lawn are a very popular attraction in the warmer months, so bring a lawn chair and settle in for an evening of quality entertainment.

POSSIBILITIES

Red/Rosé
Cab
Indian Rosé
Sweet Red

White
Greetings
Love Potion 69
Sweet Delight

Fruit
A Bell
Cran
Peachie

Hard Cider
You Are the Apple to my Pie
Peach
Cranberry
Watermelon
Cherry
Pineapple
Blueberry

TASTINGS	TAKE HOME	RESERVATIONS
4 for $3.50	$17–$29	More than 8 guests

VISIT

1261 E. Munger Rd. • Tecumseh, MI 49286

517.424.9232 • blackfirewinery.com

Open year-round

Blake's Hard Cider

ARMADA · EST. 2013

Blake's Orchard and Cider Mill is definitely a family destination, with all of the excitement you would expect of an apple orchard in the fall. But there really isn't a season when they aren't filled with visitors excited to experience all it has to offer, from its homemade baked goods to its ice-skating rink to a pick-your-own veggies opportunity. The farm has been in the family since 1946, and their commitment to a quality experience for all their visitors shows.

The tasting room is behind the front building, and its stone façade with beautiful landscaping is very inviting. Inside, the large open space provides plenty of room, its gray barnwood walls and stonework contrasting nicely with the highly polished oak bar and tables. The large outdoor veranda provides an alternative, complete with metal tables and shady umbrellas.

POSSIBILITIES

Hard Cider
Flannel Mouth
El Chavo
Grizzly Pear
Triple Jam
Strawberry Lemonade
Blueberry Lemonade
Saint Cheri
Rainbow Seeker
Caramel Apple

TASTINGS	TAKE HOME	RESERVATIONS
6 for $12	6-pack: $6–$10	Walk in

VISIT

17985 Armada Center Rd. • Armada, MI 48005

586.784.9463 • info@blakefarms.com • blakeshardcider.com

Open year-round

Bløm Meadworks

ANN ARBOR · EST. 2018

In the heart of Wolverine country, on a busy city street, the tasting room for Bløm Meadworks provides the perfect place to take a break and watch the world go by. There are other things to watch here as well; Sunday Meads + Movies is a popular event, with vintage films offering an entertaining alternative to theater chains. Board games, trivia, and comedy nights are also possibilities.

Inside, the smooth white bar extends down one side of the narrow room, while at the back, a few larger tables can seat six very comfortably. High tops fill the rest of the space. Modern murals provide a demure but colorful accent. An additional space off the front opens into a combination seating area and production facility, providing an up-close look at the tanks involved in the mead-making process. A long table runs along one side of the room, in front of a towering wall of windows, which proves a good vantage point for enjoying the bustle outside.

POSSIBILITIES
Mead
Standard
Apple Cyser
Christmas
Black Currant
Black Currant Gose
Cider
Dry Tart
Pear Ginger

TASTINGS	TAKE HOME	RESERVATIONS
4 for $11	4-pack: $12–$15	Walk in

VISIT

100 S. 4th Ave., Ste 110 • Ann Arbor, MI 48104

734.548.9729 • hello@drinkblom.com • drinkblom.com

Open year-round

Burgdorf's Winery

HASLETT · EST. 2005

The tasting room for Burgdorf's Winery is part of a private home, with a pergola overgrown with dense vines in front of the former garage. Once inside, there's a cute shop, with painted vines on the walls highlighting their motto: A Moment in Wine. The black and oak bar has plenty of room for visitors, and outside, the dappled shade of the expansive back lawn is inviting, and their large patio offers several seating areas to relax in. Huge crabapple trees stretch over the tables, and when they're in bloom, it's beautiful. If your timing is perfect, you may be able to find a bottle of the rare paw paw wine, which sells out almost immediately. The award-winning wines of Burgdorf's are brought to you courtesy of the second woman wine maker in Michigan; it's a great stop for someone interested in friendly conversation about the wines, and the industry itself.

POSSIBILITIES

Red/Rosé
Merlot
Faye
Finlay's Reserve
Wolverine Red
Marquette Reserve
Spartan Reserve

White
Un-Oaked Chardonnay
Pinot Gris
Wolverine White
Chardonnay Reserve
Vignoles
Cayuga White
Spartan White
Frontenac Blanc

Fruit
Pear
A Maize'n Blue
Strawberry-Rhubarb
Berried Treasure

TASTINGS	TAKE HOME	RESERVATIONS
4 for $10	$14–$58	For groups of 6 or more

VISIT

5635 Shoeman Rd. • Haslett, MI 48840

517.655.2883 • wine@burgdorfwinery.com • burgdorfwinery.com

Open year-round

Cellar 104

MT. CLEMENS · EST. 2019

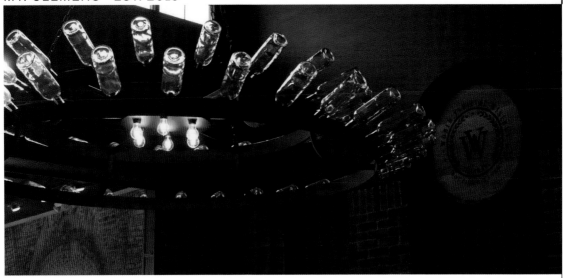

Cellar 104, the tasting room for World Varietal Winery, brings the world to you; using juices from several continents, they produce the wine locally. Inside their friendly and welcoming tasting room, large murals of vineyards and barrel rooms make you feel immersed in the experience. The large U-shaped bar has plenty of room, with many tables spread throughout the space. The large patio out front offers even more room to stretch out. Charcuterie and small plates are available, and occasional evenings of live music. For those interested in producing their own small batch of wine, they also offer a popular wine-making class. Their port is another popular item, but changes regularly; Raspberry Mocha and Toasted Caramel are a definite possibility, however.

POSSIBILITIES

Red
Cabernet Sauvignon
Pinot Noir
Merlot
Malbec
Amarone Style
Brunella

White
Riesling
Pinot Grigio
Chardonnay
Sauvignon Blanc

A Traveler's Guide to Michigan Wineries, Cideries, and Meaderies

TASTINGS	TAKE HOME	RESERVATIONS
4 for $18	$16–$36	For groups of 4 or more

VISIT

104 Macomb Place • Mt. Clemens, MI 48043

586.242.2222 • mycellar104@gmail.com • cellar104.com

Open year-round

Chalice Craft Wine

LAPEER · EST. 2003

The tasting room for Chalice Craft Winery (formerly Wills Winery) is a cozy spot created with relaxation in mind. The unique angles of their bar encourage conversation with neighbors, and the natural wood provides a warm and welcoming atmosphere. Several tables fill the space, and macramé curtains and hanging plants complete the welcoming vibe. Small charcuterie plates are also offered.

POSSIBILITIES

Red/Rosé
Black Tail Deer

White
Badger
Blonde Bear
White Swan

Fruit
Blood Orange
Blackberry Mist
Blueberry & Cream
Chocolate Cherry Red
Chocolate Raspberry Red
Peaches & Cream
Raspberry Red
Simply Psychedelic
White Rush
Wildberry Red

Ice Wine
White Diamonds
Ruby Harbor

TASTINGS	TAKE HOME	RESERVATIONS
Complimentary	$16	Walk in

VISIT

1779 W. Genesee St. · Lapeer, MI 48446

810.245.9463 · chalicewinery.com

Open year-round

Chateau Aeronautique

JACKSON · EST. 2008

W hat does a retired pilot do with all the extra space in the airplane hangar in the backyard? Make wine, of course. Aviation enthusiasts will appreciate the origin story of Aeronautique, as well as the chance to tour the facility which still houses planes in addition to the wine cellar. Inside the tasting room, a spacious glass bar rests on wine casks, while a hand-painted mural gives you a taste of the Italian countryside. Beautiful woodwork decorates a smaller room, complete with its own cozy bar usually reserved for special functions. The patio out back provides a sunny space to savor the wines as well as the cool summer breeze. Chateau Aeronautique is also affiliated with Blue Skies Brewery in the Irish Hills, and both locations have beer and cider on tap as well as wine by the glass. Concerts are a regular treat, particularly at the brewery, and have become a very popular destination for music lovers.

Blue Skies Brewery, 12000 Pentecost Hwy, Onsted, 517.446.4052;
Auburn tasting room, 3358 Auburn Hills Rd., 248.564.2710

POSSIBILITIES
Red/Rosé
Pinot Noir
Aviatrix Crimson
Syrah
Cabernet Franc
White
Dry Riesling
Sur Lie Chardonnay
Gewürztraminer
Naked Chardonnay
Semi-Sweet Riesling
Aviatrix passion
Chareau Blanc
Sweet Cabernet
Dessert
Vidal Blanc Ice Wine
Riesling Ice Wine

TASTINGS	TAKE HOME	RESERVATIONS
7 for $11 to $13	$21 to $75	Walk in

VISIT
1849 Rives Eaton Rd. · Jackson, MI 49201
517.569.2132 · Open year-round

Cherry Creek Cellars

BROOKLYN · EST. 2003

The old brick school house, complete with white shutters and school bell, has been transformed into a charming tasting room for Cherry Creek Cellars. The original wood floors have a golden glow from the tall windows surrounding the space, and the glossy bar has plenty of room for visitors. Tables are also an option, or you can venture outdoors and take in the view of the rolling fields from the patio or beneath the vine-covered pergola. Live entertainment is a regular part of the experience, with Sundays being devoted to acoustic music. Their café offers charcuterie, as well as panini, salads and wraps, but during performances the café is closed and a food truck fills in with tasty offerings.

POSSIBILITIES

Red/Rosé
Lynn Aleksandr Merlot
Lynn Aleksandr Marechal Foch
Montage
Old Schoolhouse Red
Great Lakes Nouveau
Riviera Rosé
Publican Persimmon

White
Wood Duck Riesling
Lynn Aleksandr Old Woodstock #2
Lynn Aleksandr Chardonnay
Great Lakes Old World White
La Mia Famiglia

Fruit
Cherry
Autumn Red
Cranberry Passion
Raspberry Beret

TASTINGS	TAKE HOME	RESERVATIONS
5 for $5	$13–$28	Groups of 10 or more

VISIT
11500 Silver Lake Hwy. • Brooklyn, MI 49230 • 517.592.4663
cherrycreekcellars@gmail.com • cherrycreekwine.com
Open year-round

Detroit Vineyards

DETROIT · EST. 2014

The original industrial architecture of the old Stroh's Ice Cream production facility takes center stage in what is now the home of Detroit Vineyards tasting room. From the high shelving as you walk in to the floating tables and beautiful use of stone and metal materials, the new artfully blends in with the old. Brick walls, huge production pipes and intricate bits of machinery are now showcased, with tables surrounding them as though they are works of art. The open space has plenty of room for a crowd, and is very close to Eastern Market and other downtown Detroit attractions.

POSSIBILITIES

Red
Frais
Blau
Emcee
Rosé
Cabernet Franc
Merlot
Sweet Red

White
Sauvignon Blanc
CV White Blend
Chardonnay
Semi-dry Riesling
Sweet White

Mead
Pyment
Cyser
Raspberry Melomel

TASTINGS	TAKE HOME	RESERVATIONS
Curated tasting: 5 for $20–$25	$22–$32	Strongly encouraged

VISIT
1000 Gratiot Ave. · Detroit, MI 48207
313.265.3938 · detroitvineyards.com
Open year-round

Dizzy Daisy Winery & Vineyard

BAD AXE · EST. 2006

Small but sweet, Dizzy Daisy Winery, situated in a back building on a working farm, offers a wide assortment of wines to tempt every palate. Although their tasting room is small, able to accommodate only eight comfortably, there is a front patio which offers additional seating. Their eclectic mix of fruit wines—Alpine Berry, Elderberry, Watermelon, Rhubarb—makes this a popular stop in the area.

Dizzy Daisy also has a tiny tasting room in Port Austin, at the Village Green.

POSSIBILITIES

Red/Rosé
Barnyard Red
Cabernet Sauvignon
Marquette
Noiret
Dizzy Spell
Double Dare
Five Lakes Red
Marechal Foch
Triple Dare

White
Chardonnay
Daisy Delight
Pinot Grigio
Catawba
Cayuga
Riesling
Bad Axe Passion
Dizzy Love

An Assortment of Fruit Wines

TASTINGS	TAKE HOME	RESERVATIONS
5 for $8	$8–$32	For groups over 6

VISIT

1288 Crown Rd. • Bad Axe, MI 48413
989.269.2366 • dizzydaisywinery@gmail.com • dizzydaisywinery.com
Open year-round

Dragonmead Brewery

WARREN · EST. 1997

From the front, Dragonmead is a standard issue store front, with a blue metal roof and long bench outside the front door, framed by overflowing flower pots. But once inside, visitors are treated to a space that makes the most of its old world heritage, with pennants hanging from the ceiling and stained glass windows near the bar. Although the bar itself is a bit cozy, there are plenty of tables spread throughout the large space for friends to gather. Enjoy a game of darts, or grab Settlers of Catan from the game shelf and make an afternoon of it. They offer hard cider and beer as well as wine, with small plates to accompany your tastings.

They also have a sister location, Dragon's Landing (24409 Jefferson Ave, St. Clair Shores)

POSSIBILITIES

Wine/Cider
Raspberry Peach Sangria
Strawberry Blush
White Cranberry Pinot Gris
Black Raspberry Merlot
Chardonnay
Spicy & Sweet Cider

TASTINGS
5 for $14

TAKE HOME
$20–$32

RESERVATIONS
Walk in

VISIT
14600 E. 11 Mile Rd. • Warren, MI 48089
586.776.9428 • dragonmead.com
Open year-round

Fenton Winery and Brewery

FENTON · EST. 2007

The beautiful gardens of Fenton Winery and Brewery make it a popular venue for special events, or just meeting a few special friends. The tasting room shares a large open space with the production facility; a long bar and several tables provide plenty of seating. Along with wine, they also have their beer on tap, and offer charcuterie, pizzas and sandwiches. Between the tasting room and banquet hall, a patio is dominated by a beautiful mural of flowers, and leads to the expansive gardens. Colorful vines are guided up the side of the building and strings of lights give it a festive air in the evening. A large firepit and benches are surrounded by perennials and long swathes of lawn. A small pond surrounded by a split rail fence completes the picture of a beautiful country afternoon.

POSSIBILITIES

Red/Rosé
Cocoa Merlot
Fenton Red Merlot
Mountain View Malbec
Foeder Aged Red Zin
Crimson Vine Shiraz
Solo Black Merlot
Red Forest Black Cherry
Wild Wildberry Shiraz

White
Orange Label White
Chardonnay
Hopped Up Chardonnay
Celebrate Viognier
All Sass Gewürztraminer
Moonlight Moscato

Fruit/Dessert
Breeze Pomegranate
First Frost Ice Wine
Winter Warmth

TASTINGS	TAKE HOME	RESERVATIONS
4 for $10	$21–$29	Walk in

VISIT

1370 N. Long Lake Rd. • Fenton, MI 48430

810.373.4194 • fentonbrewery.com

Open year-round

Filipo Marc Winery

CLINTON TOWNSHIP · EST. 1999

The unassuming façade of the Filipo Marc tasting room – nestled in the middle of a strip mall – hides a unique and educational wine-tasting opportunity in a very friendly space. Hand painted vines decorate the dark yellow walls, and there is a nice gift selection towards the back. Roomy tables and comfortable chairs fill the tasting area, and a small bar provides a focus for the reserved tastings that are held here. Although walk-ins are welcome if space permits, a reserved tasting ($18) includes charcuterie and a 2-hour curated experience.

POSSIBILITIES

Red/Rosé

Outback Red
The King's Choice
Bellisima
Black Tie Affair
Corazon Rojo
Royal Blend
Cabernet Shiraz
Little Italy
Black Pine

White

Outback White
Dolce D'Oro
Edelweiss
Spice of Life
Little Sister
La Mancha Ltd
Simply Sweet
Potpourri
White Pine

Assorted Fruit & Dessert Wines

TASTINGS	TAKE HOME	RESERVATIONS
Flight: 4 for $8	$12–$25	Walk in

VISIT

39085 Garfield Rd. • Clinton Township, MI 48038

586.226.3990 • fmwinery@gmail.com • filipomarcwinery.com

Open year-round

Flint City Hard Cider

FLINT EST. 2020

Flint City Hard Cider, with its gorgeous mural stretching across the side of the building, has become a gathering place for friends who love great cider and eclectic music. Long tables provide plenty of space to spread out, meet new folks, or have a lively game of euchre. Tables surround the stage area, and there is also a patio with picnic tables and strings of festive lights. Weekend food trucks are an additional attaction. Only open for a few years, it is already making waves in the cider community with several high-profile international awards.

POSSIBILITIES

Hard Cider
Fli-City Dry
La Manzana
Blossoms Up!
So Fresh & So Peach
Hoppy Boi
Heritage Blend
Berry Nana-lo
BlackBerry Buzz
Dabinette's Perfection
Dabinette's Perfection on Oak

TASTINGS	TAKE HOME	RESERVATIONS
4 for $12	Growlers: $21–$23	Walk in

VISIT

610 Martin Luther King Ave. • Flint, MI 48502

810.820.9640 • facebook.com/FlintCityHardCiderCo/

Open year-round

Flying Otter Winery

ADRIAN · EST. 2010

After following a long driveway, the road curves to the left at the edge of the vineyard, and ends in the parking area for the Flying Otter tasting room. A colorful border of zinnias outlines the weathered railing leading to the front door. Inside, the angled bar offers plenty of seats for visitors. The entire tasting room is open to the outdoors; there are several tables on the deck overlooking the vineyard, and down a short flight of stairs, picnic tables on the lawn are outlined by a split rail fence. Live music is a regular feature on weekends in the warmer months.

POSSIBILITIES
Red/Rosé
Fusion
Farrago
Frontenac
Dry Marquette Rosé
Chancellor
Marquette
Curmudgeon's Red
Rachis Ruckus
Intrigue
Bazinga
Sexy Devil
Marquette Sweet Rosé
White
Curmudgeon's White
Northern Lights
Riesling
St. Pepin
Brianna

TASTINGS	TAKE HOME	RESERVATIONS
6 for $6	$11–$32	Walk in

VISIT

3402 Chase Rd. · Adrian, MI 49221

567.302.0476 · info@flyingotter.com · flyingotter.com

Open seasonally

Fourth Coast Ciderworks

LAKE ORION · 2017

The cheery white and red tasting room of Fourth Coast Ciderworks is housed in an old stable, with several of the original fixtures still intact. An assortment of seating areas for groups of all sizes are scattered throughout the rooms. Each area is a cozy retreat from the hustle and bustle outside. The tasting room is part of Canterbury Village, a collection of unique shops and a venue for festive events throughout the year. It's a very popular destination for families, and the shady entrance to Fourth Coast can be very attractive. There are weekly movie music trivia nights, and live music is an occasional treat.

POSSIBILITIES

Hard Cider
Rooted Insanity
Wildflower
Crazy Cassie
Citrus Session
Fourth Coast Jamboree
Smoke 'N Stout
D-HOP-T
Hopricot
Prickly Peach
Bavarian Hefe-Cider
Winter Wonderland
Spruce Lee
Dragon's Breath
Maddie's Madness

TASTINGS	TAKE HOME	RESERVATIONS
Varies	4-pack $16-$28	Walk in

2356 Joslyn Ct. • Lake Orion, MI 48360
947.300.6016 • fourthcoastciderworks.com
Open seasonally

Green Barn Winery

SMITH'S CREEK · EST. 2012

If you are looking for a collection of sulfite-free wine, you won't want to miss Green Barn Winery. The friendly atmosphere at the large green tasting room is very welcoming, and visitors will want to sit a spell on the wide front porch or on the covered patio, its corrugated metal roof styled like a farm silo. There's a fire pit for the cooler months, or you can find a seat inside near the fireplace. The barstools are equipped with saddles to add a bit of fun. The gift shop has plenty of tasty items as well as cute wine-theme gifts, and weekends include a selection of tempting desserts.

POSSIBILITIES

Red/Rosé

Tuscan
Nebbiolo
Shiraz
Cabernet Sauvignon
Grand Merlot
Harvester Red
Wadhams Red
Barnyard Red

White

Pink Lace
Dry Summer Night
White Zinfandel
Piesporter
Back Woods Chardonnay
Gewürztraminer
Riesling
Morning Mist

TASTINGS	TAKE HOME	RESERVATIONS
5 for $7	$13–$17	Walk in

VISIT

775 Wadhams Rd. • Smith's Creek, MI 48074

810.367.2400 • greenbarnwinery@hotmail.com • greenbarnwinery.com

Open seasonally

Hoffman Farms Winery

HIGHLAND · EST. 2016

Horse lovers will gravitate to Hoffman Farms tasting room, which shares its space with an equine training facility and boarding area. The stately white tasting room—complete with columns stretching two stories along its wide front porch—dominates its surroundings. The deep green pastures are bordered by black fences and dotted with horses; the front porch is the perfect place for visitors to get a close up look at these beautiful animals as they are taken out or returned to their stalls after a ride. Inside, the cozy yellow tasting room has space for eight to sit at the bar, and there are several tables surrounding it. Small plates are available. There is the added treat of a window overlooking the inside of the training facility, where you can watch riders hone their craft.

There are no pets allowed at this facility.

POSSIBILITIES

Red/Rosé
Pinot Noir
Reserve Marquette
Maverick Red
Farm House Red

White
Pinot Gris
Cheval Blanc
Farm House White
Unbridled

Fruit
Rose Center Blackberry
Rose Center Cherry

Hard Cider
Apple Blackberry
Apple Cherry
Cinnamon Apple
Cranberry Apple
Peach
Raspberry

TASTINGS	TAKE HOME	RESERVATIONS
5 for $12	$15–$25	Walk in

VISIT

2521 Rose Center Rd. • Highland, MI 48356 • 248.714.5953
leanne@rjhoffmanmanagement.com
facebook.com/HoffmanFarmsWinery
Open year-round

Howell's Main Street Winery

HOWELL · EST. 2008

A tasting room with an inviting stretch of sidewalk tables beneath a shady canopy, Howell's Main Street Winery is the perfect place to end an afternoon of shopping, or just stop in for a taste. Inside, the long, narrow room is filled with gifts up front, and a polished wooden bar stretching the length of the space and contrasting with the exposed brick walls. Opposite the bar, large wooden tables provide space for groups of friends to gather. It's also a pizzeria offering delicious stone oven fare, salads, and appetizers including baked Brie. Chandeliers and strings of lights criss-crossing the room give it a playful vibe.

POSSIBILITIES

Red/Rosé
Main Street Rosay
Salute!
Tango Red
Amerone Italian Red
Luna Rossa
Village Cellar Red

White
Dolci Momenti
City of Light
Beethoven's Finest
Menagerie
Over the Moon
House White
Bella
Spe Salvi

Fruit/Dessert
First Sin
Very Blueberry
VuDu
Sangria
Sweet Decadence

TASTINGS	TAKE HOME	RESERVATIONS
Complimentary	$14–$22	Walk in

VISIT

201 W. Grand River Ave. • Howell, MI 48843

517.545.9463 • johnandsandy@howellsmainstreetwinery.com

howellsmainstreetwinery.com

Open year-round

JK's Farmhouse Ciders

FLUSHING · EST. 1860

At Mar Orchards market, a white metal building which houses an assortment of tasty offerings from organic popcorn to jams and jellies, is the home of JK's Farmhouse Ciders. Tastings are in the back room, which has a small bar but a very friendly atmosphere. Many of their ciders are organic, which makes them very popular. If you want a taste of the exotic, Michigan-style, go for the Patriotic Paw-Paw, which is a rare fruit native to the area. The market is in the middle of their orchards, and when fall hits, it can become very busy. Hay rides, fresh doughnuts, and pumpkins galore!

POSSIBILITIES

Hard Cider
Scrumpy
Northern Neighbor
The Pair
Winterruption
Rosé
Honeycrisp Haze
Farmhouse Summer
Patriotic Paw Paw
Traverse City Cherry

TASTINGS	TAKE HOME	RESERVATIONS
Complimentary	4-pack: $11	Walk in

VISIT

1431 Duffield Rd. • Flushing, MI 48433

810.659.6568 • jksfarmhouseciders.com

Open year-round

McCallum's Orchard and Cider Mill

JEDDO · EST. 2017

A country lane, lined with a canopy of trees, guides visitors to the welcoming red and white farm market of McCallum's Orchard and Cider Mill. A shady lawn leads to the entrance, with picnic tables dotting the covered front patio. Inside, a large gift shop with a wide assortment of ciders, honey, and fresh baked goods is a popular stop. In the back, a larger area is home to the tasting room. There is a small bar, and an assortment of tables inside. Autumn days are filled with visitors to the petting zoo and pumpkin patch. Younger guests can blow off some steam by climbing a mountain made of straw, or winding their way through either the sunflower or corn maze.

POSSIBILITIES

Fruit
Cherry
Blackberry
Apple
Pear
Peach
Blueberry
Concord Grape

TASTINGS
5 for $7

TAKE HOME
$15

RESERVATIONS
Walk in

VISIT

5697 Harris Rd. • Jeddo, MI 48032
810.887.8774 • mccallumsorchard.com
Open seasonally

Meckley's Flavor Fruit Farm

CEMENT CITY · 1956

The tasting room for Meckley's Cellars is upstairs in a large gray barn-style building complete with gambrel roof. The entrance is shaded by a pergola covered with thick vines; there are a few chairs arranged beneath it. Inside, you'll be hard pressed to resist the very popular baked goods on your way upstairs to the tasting room. The bar is small, but there is plenty of room at the mismatched tables and chairs throughout the space. Outdoors, there is a deck with pergola and vines overhead; it's shady but not weatherproof, so you may have to shelter inside. Meckley's offers a variety of drinks, from wines to hard cider and even beer. Dog lovers will enjoy the geometric portraits on each wine label; several breeds are highlighted in this modern technique. Fall is definitely their high season, and a family can spend an afternoon testing out the corn maze, picking out a pumpkin, or just taking a stroll with a fresh glass of cider and a warm cinnamon sugar doughnut.

POSSIBILITIES

Red/Rosé
Merlot Reserve
Meritage
Amstaff Rosé
Apollo Red
Bristol Noir

White/Fruit
Chardonnay Reserve
Empress
Sparkling Riesling
Boxwood Riesling
Spiced Haven & Honey
Ice Wine

TASTINGS	TAKE HOME	RESERVATIONS
5 for $5	$13–$24	Walk in
	4-pack: $15	

VISIT

11025 S, Jackson Rd. • Cement City, MI 49233

517.688.3455 • meckleyevents@gmail.com • flavorfruitfarm.com

Open year-round

Northville Winery and Brewing Co.

NORTHVILLE · EST. 1982

clectic art, old school arcade games, and live music are what keeps fans coming back to Northville Winery tasting room. And the libations, of course. The huge red barn with its shady lawn is the perfect place for outdoor concerts; picnic tables dot the area, and food trucks are a regular feature. Inside, the small tasting bar has an assortment of ever-changing wines, ciders and beers, which are all produced in-house. There is plenty of seating at the tables surrounding the bar, and the arcade games will be hard to resist. In the fall, the cider mill next door offers tasty baked goods and fresh-pressed ciders.

POSSIBILITIES

Hard Cider
Rockin' Cock
Crimson Dew
Blueriver
Baseline Brut
Wallflower
Cockadeus
Infrared Vibrations
Juniper
Red
Sangiovese

TASTINGS	TAKE HOME	RESERVATIONS
3 for $6	$8–$10	Walk in

VISIT

630 Baseline Rd. · Northville, MI 48167

248.320.6507 • northvillewinery@gmail.com • thenorthvillewinery.com

Open year-round

Owl Wineries

ROSEVILLE · EST. 2017

The small brick tasting room, with its picture windows and gray awning, makes Owl Wineries a perfect spot for a cozy sip and friendly conversation. The bar seats four, but there is an eclectic assortment of chairs and tables arranged throughout the space. Their fruit wines do not contain grapes, making their creations unique in the wine world. Everything is created on-site with the best Michigan has to offer.

POSSIBILITIES

Fruit
Sweet Apple
Blackberry
Strawberry
Brooze
Chapple Rosé
Cherry
Dry Harvest Apple
Raspberry
Blueberry

TASTINGS	TAKE HOME	RESERVATIONS
4 for $8	$17	Walk in

VISIT

28087 Gratiot Ave. · Roseville, MI 48066

586.272.6514 · owlwineries@gmail.com · owlwineries.com

Open year-round

Pentamere Winery

TECUMSEH · EST. 2002

A long a strip of vintage downtown buildings, Pentamere Winery has found a home. The front windows fill the space with light, helped along by the bright yellow walls. Exposed brick and original wood floors are a throwback to the building's history as a dry goods store and upstairs dance hall. But the center of the room has a unique attraction. Visitors can peer into the basement production facility through the large opening cut in the floor, where stainless steel vats poke up through the space. Stop by for a friendly tasting at the bar, and browse through their gourmet offerings to serve at your next get-together.

POSSIBILITIES

Red/Rosé
Idle Hour
Keepsake
Cascaden Cabernet Sauvignon
Watchawana Blush
Channel Marker Two

White
Wings of the Wind
Morning Star
Lady of the Lakes
May Wine
Channel Marker Three

Fruit/Specialty
Harvest Apple
Midnight Plum
Black berry
Baked Apple

TASTINGS	TAKE HOME	RESERVATIONS
1 for $1-$2	$14–$25	Walk in

VISIT

131 E. Chicago Blvd. • Tecumseh, MI 49286 • 517.423.9000
pentamerewinerytecumseh@gmail.com • pentamerewinery.com
Open year-round

Sage Creek Winery

MEMPHIS · EST. 2013

The stately brown brick building, a 19th century classic, has found new life as the tasting room for Sage Creek Winery. The entrance is framed with columns and crowned with an arched window, and inside much of its beautiful woodwork has been left intact. The front room boasts a fireplace and comfy leather seating arrangement, while in the room beyond, the live-edge bar and wooden tables provide plenty of space for friends to meet up . Outside, a beautiful paved patio, complete with timber-framed walls open to the breezes of summer, becomes an enclosed and cozy space in the winter, with a large fireplace dominating one end of the structure. On weekends, food trucks provide popular treats for guests, making it a great place to unwind after a long week.

POSSIBILITIES
Red
Cherry Bomb
Strawberry Bon Bon
Blueberry Muffin
Memphis Belle
Blackberry Beauty
Blood Orange
White
Hunter's Widow
That's My Jam
Playing with Fire
Caribbean Queen
White Cranberry
Somewhere on a Beach
Bee's Knees
Weekend White
Cabin Fever
Specialty
Salted Caramel
Campfire S'Mores
Coffee Port

TASTINGS	TAKE HOME	RESERVATIONS
4 for $12	$14–$21	Walk in

VISIT
35050 Bordman Rd. • Memphis, MI 48041
810.392.5007 • sagecreekmi@gmail.com • sagecreekmi.com
Open year-round

Sandhill Crane Vineyards

JACKSON · EST. 2003

From the shady front lawn to the wide covered porch, there is ample opportunity to stretch out and relax, gazing out over the tidy green rows of the vineyards which surround the tasting room of Sandhill Crane Vineyards. Inside, exposed beams call attention to the row of windows overhead, creating a bright and open space filled with a large bar and plenty of seating areas. A fireplace provides an interesting touch, while French doors lead out to the patio. Glass-framed fireplace tables take the chill off the cool spring and autumn days, and their cafe has a small but interesting menu—smoked trout spread, pesto torta—which changes regularly. Visitors are welcome to bring their own chairs and relax on the lawn or beneath the vine-covered pergola, particularly on the weekends, when live music and food trucks create a festive atmosphere. For the more energetic guest, the vineyard sponsors an annual 5K and half-marathon which runs through the vineyard.

POSSIBILITIES

Red/Rosé
Sassy Rosé
Merlot
Abrazo
Night of the Living Red
Revenge of the Living Red
After Sundown
Rhapsody in Red

White
Proprietor's Reserve Traminette
Vintner's Select Riesling
Vignoles
Sauvignon Blanc
Pinot Blanc
Sur Lie Chardonnay
Pinot Grigio
Vidal Blanc
Riesling

Mead
Blue Skies
Veranda
Raspberry Bourbon Barrel Reserve

Dessert
Annie's Mapleshine
Dolce
Dolce Bourbon Barrel Reserve
Raspberry
Sunday Blues
Port

TASTINGS	TAKE HOME	RESERVATIONS
4 for $12	$15–$30	For groups over 6

VISIT

4724 Walz Rd. • Jackson, MI 49201 • 517.764.0679

winemaker@sandhillcranevineyards.com • sandhillcranevineyards.com

Open year-round

Spicer's Winery

FENTON · EST. 2009

The white colonial tasting room, complete with cupolas, clapboard siding and a cut stone foundation, brings a sense of history to Spicer's Winery. Inside, the room is spacious but still cozy, with pine accents and a display of antique grape presses and kettles. Framed red scrollwork decorates the bar, while wrought iron chairs and tables provide a rest from the hectic day. Or have a seat on the shady back porch overlooking the orchards and the activities for visitors. The tasting room for Spicer's Winery is part of a larger complex which includes their cider mill and farm market, both of which deserve a visit. In the fall, celebrations happen daily and make a visit to Spicer's an absolute must for many area residents. Activities for families include picking your own fruit, a corn maze, wagon rides, and farm animals to view.

POSSIBILITIES

Red/Rosé
Merlot
Pinot Noir
Carriage Dry Red
Red Demi-Sec
House Red
Soft Red

White
Pinot Grigio
Cabernet Sauvignon
White Demi-Sec
Traminette
Sweet Riesling
Moscato
Niagara
Catawba

Fruit
Blueberry
Cherry
Sangria
Red Currant
Cranberry
Raspberry
Sparkling Peach
Honey & White

TASTINGS
4 for $8

TAKE HOME
$16–$23

RESERVATIONS
Walk in

VISIT

10411 Clyde Rd. · Fenton, MI 48430

810.632.7692 · spicerswinery@gmail.com · spicerswinery.com

Open year-round

Superior Lakes Mead, Wine and Cider

HARRISON TOWNSHIP · EST. 2011

There is something for everyone in this tasting room, as Superior Lakes offers the trifecta of wine, mead, and hard cider. Their cute blue and white building is close to the bay, just across the street from the marina. Picnic tables are lined up in a sunny spot in front of the building; inside, the small bar seats six comfortably, and informal seating creates a cozy spot to relax with friends. Their creativity is apparent in the specialty drinks they've created by mixing their own wares—try a Denmark Donkey or The Ascot Incident. They offer charcuterie and N/A drinks as well.

POSSIBILITIES

Mead
White
Barrel Aged
Pear Pyment
Dark Cherry Pyment
Motorboat
Tropic Like It's Hot
Cream Soda-ish
Vern's Oars
Spiceberries

Wine
Festival White
Red Dragon
Festival Red
Peep
Strawberry Roundhouse
Healing Potion
Monkfruit Cherry

Cider
Scurvy Dog
Ivan the Perrible

TASTINGS	TAKE HOME	RESERVATIONS
5 for $9	$9–$40	Walk in

VISIT

36285 Jefferson Ave. • Harrison Township, MI 48045

586.231.9501 • info@superiorlakes.com • superiorlakes.com

Open year-round

Tennerra Winery

STERLING HEIGHTS · EST. 2017

Hidden in plain sight, the tasting room for Tennerra Winery (originally Buon Amici) is in a low-key industrial park, sharing a building with Macomb Vintner Supply. The tasting room offers a large granite bar and plenty of seating throughout. On weekends, they fire up the pizza oven and invite visitors to stay for a bite to eat. The friendly hosts and cozy atmosphere make it a popular spot to spend a few hours in relaxing conversation.

POSSIBILITIES

Red/Rosé
Bordeau Style Blend
Cabernet
Malbec
Meritage
Merlot
Nebbiolo
Pinot Noir
Sweet Merlot
Syrah
Tre Rossi
Zinfandel

White
Moscato
Blanco Secco
Chardonnay
Gewürztraminer
Moscato
Pinot Grigio
Sauvignon Blanc
Tre Bianchi

Dessert
Black Forest
Chocolate
Raspberry
Late Harvest Riesling
Toasted Caramel
White Chocolate

Fruit
Acai Raspberry
Black Raspberry
Pomegranate
Raspberry
Sangria
Watermelon

TASTINGS
5 for $15

TAKE HOME
$12–$18

RESERVATIONS
Walk in

VISIT
44443 Phoenix Dr. • Sterling Heights, MI 48314
586.884.7868 • inquiry@tennerra.com • tennerra.com
Open year-round

Two Rivers Winery

MARINE CITY · EST. 2021

The green and black tasting room for Two Rivers Winery is in the middle of a city block of storefronts overlooking the St. Clair River, just a few blocks from where the Belle River joins it. Inside, a decorative ceiling, a wooden floor polished to a high gloss, and black accents throughout combine to create a warm ambiance. The rough-cut wooden bar seats over eight, and there are plenty of tables for the overflow. A charcuterie board is an option, and it's a pleasant place to sit and watch the river flow past Canada on the opposite bank. For a closer look, visit the park along the riverbank just across the street, which is also home to the Peche Island Rear Range Light.

POSSIBILITIES

Red/Rosé
Old Town Merlot
Swan Shiraz
Cabernet Sauvignon
Pinot Noir
Deep Red Malbec
River Rd. Rosé
Lighthouse
Nebbliolo
Merlot
Cab Merlot
Cab Shiraz

White
Moscato
Artisan Riesling
The Pinot Pickerel
Gewürztraminer
White Zinfandel
Traminer Riesling
Pathfinder Sauvignon Blanc

Dessert/Specialty
Dessert Wine
Dessert Port
Hard Cherry

Fruit
Sinfull Strawberry
Caramel Apple
Marine City Mule
Prickly Pear
Anglers Apple
Water Street White Cranberry
Mariner Blood Orange
Bold Tart Cherry
Boathouse Blueberry

TASTINGS	TAKE HOME	RESERVATIONS
$12	$15–$28	Walk in

VISIT

218 S. Water St. • Marine City, MI 48039 • 810.420.0604

tworiverswinerymc@gmail.com • 2riverswinery.com

Open year-round

Uncle John's Cider Mill

ST. JOHNS · EST. 2003

On a small hill above the highway, Uncle John's is a can't-miss attraction, with the roof of the huge white barn emblazoned with its name. The entrance to the tap room is towards the south of the complex, in a cute white clapboard building with red trim. Its covered porch has its own bar for busy days, and benches and tables are scattered about. Inside, the friendly tasting room is very cozy, with a small bar and several tables. This is a very popular place, so plan your visit accordingly. You can either revel in the weekend excitement, or immerse yourself in the relative quiet of a weekday. Summer offers craft shows and music festivals, while the fall offers everything a cider mill should—warm doughnuts, fresh cider, carnivals, a petting zoo, pumpkins, tours of the orchards via wagon or on your own, and their intricate fall corn maze.

POSSIBILITIES

Hard Cider
Apple
Apple Cherry
Apple Pear
Apple Blueberry
Apple Apricot
Apple Cranberry
Atomic Apple
Blossom
Raspberry Rosé

Red
Harvest Red
Concord

White
Fruithouse White
Pyment
Nectar

Fruit/Specialty
Cranberry
Fruit Harvest Cherry
Sparkling Harvest Peach

TASTINGS	TAKE HOME	RESERVATIONS
6 complimentary	$12–$18	Walk in

VISIT

8614 N. U.S. 127 · St. Johns, MI 48879

989.224.3686 · cider@ujcidermill.com · ujcidermill.com

Open seasonally

Unwined Winery

SHELBY TOWNSHIP · EST. 2019

Tucked into the corner of a strip mall on a busy city street, Unwined is a peaceful oasis where visitors can meet up with friends or stop by on the spur of the moment. The comfortable seating area, complete with fireplace, and spacious bar provide a friendly and relaxing space to sample their wares. Cozy outdoor seating in front provides a shady alternative. They also offer a charcuterie board, salads, gourmet popcorn and a delicious assortment of flatbreads.

POSSIBILITIES

Red/Rosé
Crowd Pleaser
Onyx
Miss Scarlet
Crimson
Proud Meri
Blackbird

White
Great White
Mac Daddy
Parana
Simple Elegance
California Cat
Sensation
Perfection
Celebration

Specialty/Dessert
Fire in the Hole Jalapeño
Orange Chocolate Port
Toasted Caramel Port
Raspberry Mocha Port

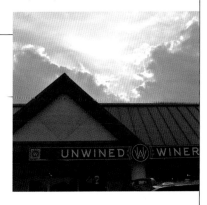

TASTINGS	TAKE HOME	RESERVATIONS
6 for $10	$13–$35	Walk in

VISIT

47653 Van Dyke Ave. • Shelby Township, MI 48317

586.932.2600 • info@uwwinery.com • uwwinery.com

Open year-round

Vine-N-Berry Winery

BAD AXE · EST. 2011

Tucked beneath a shady tree and surrounded by flowers, the tiny tasting room of Vine-N-Berry is something out of a story book. A stone walkway leads to the entrance of the green-trimmed cottage, where planters of colorful annuals spill over and a few chairs invite you to sit and enjoy a little country enchantment. Inside, the friendly and welcoming atmosphere is enticing, and the eclectic décor warrants a closer look. It's a unique and diminutive take on the traditional tasting room, and well worth the visit.

POSSIBILITIES

Fruit
Rhubarb
Strawberry
Pear
Tomato
Apple
Blueberry
Strawberry
Plum
Red Grape
Cran-Grape
Peach
Banana
Pineapple
Cranberry
Raspberry
Blackberry

TASTINGS	TAKE HOME	RESERVATIONS
5 for $5	$18	Walk in

VISIT

3475 Stein Rd. • Bad Axe, MI 48413

989.551.1616 • vinenberry.com

Open seasonally

Vinomondo Winery

FORT GRATIOT · EST. 2004

The tasting room of Vinomondo Winery brings the world to your table by offering wines created using juices from around the globe. There is plenty of room throughout the separate areas of the tasting room, and the rustic décor gives it a relaxing and welcoming vibe. They also offer pizzas and charcuterie, or you can mix and match items for a personal picnic basket of snacks. Personalization services are also offered for their wines. You can pick out your favorite, or create your own combination, and have them bottle it up with a personalized label. They are very friendly and generous with their winemaking knowledge; if the idea strikes your fancy, the extensive gift shop also offers supplies for the home winemaker as well, with a starter package at about $100.

POSSIBILITIES

Red/Rosé

Lodi Old Vine Zinfandel
Ranch II Cabernet Sauvignon
Sonoma Valley Pinot Noir
Napa Valley Stag's Leap Merlot
Australian Shiraz
Chilean Malbec

White

Washington State Riesling
New Zealand Sauvignon Blanc
Australian Chardonnay
Chilean Chardonnay
Italian Pinot Grigio
South African Chenin Blanc

Fruit

Pomegranate Zinfandel
Black Raspberry Merlot
Strawberry White Merlot
Green Apple Riesling

TASTINGS	TAKE HOME	RESERVATIONS
8 for $5	$9–$16	Walk in

VISIT

4505 Lakeshore Rd. • Fort Gratiot, MI 48059

810.384.4062 • wine@vinomondowinery.com • vinomondowinery.com

Open year-round

Washington Street Wine House

NEW BALTIMORE · EST. 2010

The Washington St. Wine House is a narrow two-story building with the charm of yesterday—black awnings stretching over large front windows, an oak front door with transom overhead—but mixed with a few modern updates. Filling the space with unique gift items and their cork-covered bar, they've made sure there's something for everyone in this cozy space. Less than a block from the tasting room is an inviting park and pier overlooking Anchor Bay and the small islands dotting the mouth of the St. Clair River.

POSSIBILITIES
Red/Rosé
Scandalous
Drop Dead Red
Rumor
Red Stiletto
Petit Red
Tango Red
Bella Ciao
House Red Blend
White
Oakey Blonde
Petit White
Washington Street White
Midnight Rendezvous
Fruit
Razzie Red
Seasonal Red
Twilight Mist
Enchanted
Water Tower White
Landmark

TASTINGS	TAKE HOME	RESERVATIONS
Complimentary	$14–$18	Walk in

VISIT
50969 Washington St. • New Baltimore, MI 48047
586.273.7140 • wswh@comcast.net • washingtonstreetwinehouse.com
Open year-round

Westview Orchards and Winery

WASHINGTON · EST. 2016

In the summer and fall, Westview Orchards stations their tasting room on the porch of their white schoolhouse, where a cute picket fence borders a group of picnic tables and shady umbrellas. Relax in the shade and enjoy the country ambiance. In the winter, tastings are moved to the top floor of the cider barn, providing a warm and spacious area to sample their wares. The bar has plenty of room for visitors, and cute seating arrangements stretch the length of the room. Strings of lights highlight the beauty of the rafters overhead; who needs farmhouse chic when you have the real thing all around you?

Westview Orchards is an interesting place to visit throughout the year. Live music on select weekends, line dancing, and the farm market and bakery are just a few of the things to enjoy. Summer includes wagon rides, farm animals and sunflowers. In the fall, events are in full swing and include many perennial favorites, such as pick-your-own fruits, a pumpkin patch, and fresh cider and doughnuts.

POSSIBILITIES
Red/Rosé
Berry Blues
Catawba
Sweet Revenge
Cranberry Crush
Hot Rod
Maybe Yes – Maybe No
Romeo Red
White
Awesome Apple
Jammin' Juice
Peach Queen
Rockin' Raspberry
Girl's Best Friend
Day at the Beach
Stolen Kiss
Strawberry Dreamin'
Summer Breeze
Wine der Woman
Hard Ciders on tap

TASTINGS	TAKE HOME	RESERVATIONS
3 for $8	$16–$24	Walk in

VISIT

65075 Van Dyke • Washington, MI 48095 • 586.752.3123
westviewromeoevents@gmail.com • westvieworchards.com
Open seasonally

Whole Hearted Winery

NEW HUDSON · EST. 2019

The beautiful green 1920s home on Grand River is a popular stop for many visitors; they are enticed not just by the wines, but also the very friendly and welcoming ambiance surrounding the Whole Hearted Winery tasting room. The red entrance door, sheltered beneath a columned portico, leads to a minimalist interior, with exposed beams and brick. There are plenty of seats at the bar and surrounding tables, or you can have a seat on the patio outside. Live music is a regular feature, and they offer a variety of events throughout the year. The winery also puts their money where their heart is: into the community. For every bottle sold, $1 is donated to local causes.

POSSIBILITIES

Red/Rosé
Raspberry Rosé
Black Cherry
Black & Blue
Black Raspberry Merlot
Pomegranate Wildberry Zinfandel
Dragonfly Red
Sangiovese
Petit Verdot
Zinfandel
Rosé
Merlot Italian
3 Hearts

White
Raspberry Peach Sangria
Green Apple Riesling
Peach Chardonnay
White Cranberry
Treasure

TASTINGS	TAKE HOME	RESERVATIONS
4 for $8	$11–$14	Walk in

VISIT

56808 Grand River Ave., Bldg. A • New Hudson, MI 48165

248.667.8441 • hello@winethatgives.com • winethatgives.com

Open year-round

The Winery North of 12

BROOKLYN · EST. 2020

Tucked in at the back of an open field, framed by pines and overhanging oaks, the tasting room of The Winery North of 12 is a popular and friendly country retreat. Weekends are filled with live music on the patio, red umbrellas and strings of lights adding to the festive atmosphere. Inside, inlaid pinstriping adds a finishing touch to the roomy bar, and there are plenty of tables for groups of friends to gather. The beautiful artwork over the bar is the perfect finishing touch. As an extra enticement to visit, they've started brewing beer as well.

POSSIBILITIES
Red/Rosé
Meritage
Merlot
Trajectory
Vino Rubino
Crimson Glow
North of 12
Currant Locale
White
Ivory Swan
Ascencions
White Willow

TASTINGS
5 for $7

TAKE HOME
$14–$28

RESERVATIONS
Walk in

VISIT
12775 Knapp Rd. • Brooklyn, MI 49320
517.592.5909 • info@northof12.com • northof12.com
Open year-round

Youngblood Vineyard

RAY · EST. 2016

The "tasting room" for Youngblood Vineyards is an outdoor area next to the vineyard, and includes a beautifully tiled pizza oven, a spacious bar, and plenty of seating throughout. Choose a spot on the couches beneath the pergola and relax, enjoying the antics of the goats in the pen across the drive. If you crave an even closer connection with nature, sign up for one of their unique classes— Tiny Goat Yoga. But don't be fooled by the cute distractions - wine is still front and center at Youngblood, and the proof of their talent is in the awards they've garnered. Their Marquette has recently won best in class in the Michigan Wine Competition, and they are consistently voted favorite winery in the Detroit area. Youngblood Vineyards is the happy place for lots of people, but nobody loves it more than the owners' son, who has a YouTube channel under the name "vine boy." If you need regular updates about what's going on in this little slice of heaven, it's only a click away.

POSSIBILITIES
Red/Rosé
Rose of Petite Pearl
Petite Pearl
Marquette
White
Frontenac Blanc
Sherman Blanc

TASTINGS	TAKE HOME	RESERVATIONS
6 for $10	$18–$25	Walk in

VISIT

61829 Ray Center Rd. • Ray, MI 48096 • 586.770.5220

jyoungblood@youngbloodvineyard.com • youngbloodvineyard.com

Open year-round

Distilleries of Southeast Michigan

Alévri Mill Distilling Co.

148 W. Michigan Ave., Clinton, MI 49236

517.456.5624

Vodka, Rum, Gin

American Fifth Spirits

112 N Larch St., Lansing, MI 48912

517.999.2631

Whiskey, Gin, Vodka

Ann Arbor Distilling Company

220 Felch St., Ann Arbor, Mi 48103

734.882.2169

Gin, Vodka, Whiskey, Schnapps, Liqueur, Absinthe

Detroit City Distillery

2462 Riopelle, Detroit, MI 48207

313.656.4528

Whiskey, Vodka, Gin

Ellison Brewery and Spirits

4903 Dawn Ave., East Lansing, MI 48823

517.203.5498

Whiskey, Vodka, Gin, Rum

Griffin Claw Brewing Company

575 S. Eton St., Birmingham, MI 48009

248.712.4050

Vodka, Gin, Rum, Whiskey, Schnapps

MichiGrain Distillery

523 E. Shiawassee St., Lansing, MI 48912

517.220.0560

Vodka, Whiskey, Gin, Rum

Motor City Gas Whiskey

325 E. 4th St., Royal Oak, MI 48067

248.599.1427

Whiskey

Red Cedar Spirits

2000 Merritt Rd., East Lansing, MI 48823

517.908.9950

Whiskey, Gin, Vodka, Brandy

Rusted Crow Spirits

6056 N. Telegraph Rd., Dearborn Heights, MI

313.551.4164

Moonshine, Gin, Whiskey, Rum, Vodka

Sanctuary Spirits

902 E. Saginaw Hwy, Grand Ledge, MI 48837

517.925.1930

Gin, Rum, Vodka, Whiskey, Liqueur

Two James Spirits

2445 Michigan Ave., Detroit, MI 48216

(also tasting room in Grand Rapids – 740
Michigan St. NE, Grand Rapids, MI 49503)

313.964.4800

Whiskey, Gin, Rum, Vodka, Absinthe

Ugly Dog Distillery

218 S. Main St., Chelsea, MI 48118

734.433.0433

Bourbon, Rum, Vodka, Gin

Uncle John's Fruit House Distillery

(at Uncle John's Cider Mill)

8614 N. US 127, St. Johns, MI 48879

989.224.3686

Vodka, Apple Brandy

Valentine Distilling Co.

161 Vester Ave., Ferndale, MI 48220

248.628.9951

Whiskey

Index